GLENCOE
Backpack Reader

COURSE **2** BOOK 1

WITH A
GRAPHIC NOVEL
IN EVERY UNIT!

www.glencoe.com

Glencoe

New York, New York   Columbus, Ohio   Chicago, Illinois   Peoria, Illinois   Woodland Hills, California

Acknowledgments

Grateful acknowledgment is given authors, publishers, photographers, museums, and agents for permission to reprint the following copyrighted material. Every effort has been made to determine copyright owners. In case of any omissions, the Publisher will be pleased to make suitable acknowledgments in future editions.
Acknowledgments continued on page R2.

 **Glencoe**

The McGraw-Hill Companies

Send all inquiries to:
Glencoe/McGraw-Hill
8787 Orion Place
Columbus, OH 43240-4027
ISBN-13: 978-0-07-874334-4
ISBN-10: 0-07-874334-6
Printed in the United States of America.

2 3 4 5 6 7 8 9 110/055 10 09 08 07 06

Table of Contents

Table of Contents

UNIT **4** Who influences us and how do they do so? _____ 204

UNIT 1
BIG Question

Why do we read?

They are everywhere you look: on signs, in newspapers and magazines, on video games and television, and game instructions, in books, and on the Internet. **What are they? Words! Why do we read?** *We read for information, entertainment, adventure—to learn and to enjoy!*

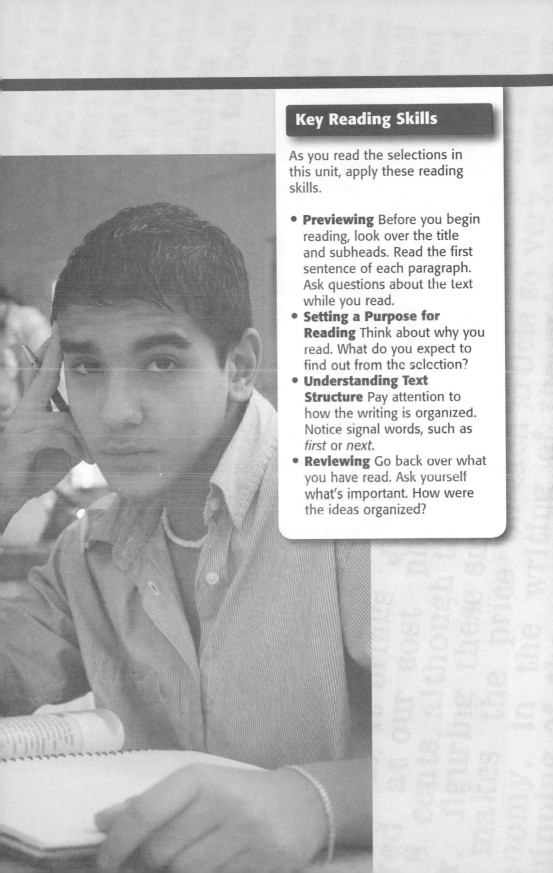

Key Reading Skills

As you read the selections in this unit, apply these reading skills.

- **Previewing** Before you begin reading, look over the title and subheads. Read the first sentence of each paragraph. Ask questions about the text while you read.
- **Setting a Purpose for Reading** Think about why you read. What do you expect to find out from the selection?
- **Understanding Text Structure** Pay attention to how the writing is organized. Notice signal words, such as *first* or *next*.
- **Reviewing** Go back over what you have read. Ask yourself what's important. How were the ideas organized?

THE CALAMITY KIDS IN:

THE BERMUDA TRIANGLE TERRARIUM!

by Jerzy Drozd and Sara Turner

Reading is the key to solving a dangerous mystery in the fourth dimension.

9

WRITE TO LEARN
Think about the ways reading could save your life in the real world. List them in your Learner's Notebook.

to young readers

by Gwendolyn Brooks

Grab a key to the treasures that are hidden in books.

Good books are
bandages
and voyages
and <u>linkages</u> to Light;

are keys and hammers,
ripe <u>redeemers</u>,
dials and bells and
healing <u>hallelujah</u>.

Good books are good nutrition.
A reader is a Guest
nourished, by riches of the Feast,
to lift, to launch, and to applaud
      the world.

Vo•cab•u•lary

linkages (LING kij ez) connections
redeemers (rih DEE murz) rescuers
hallelujah (hal eh LOO ya) an expression of joy

INVITATION

by Shel Silverstein

What are you invited to do?

If you are a dreamer, come in,
If you are a dreamer, a wisher, a liar,
A hope-er, a pray-er, a magic bean buyer...
If you're a pretender, come sit by my fire
For we have some <u>flax</u>-golden tales to spin.
Come in!
Come in!

Answering the BIG Question

As you do the following activities, consider the Big Question:
Why do we read?

WRITE TO LEARN Think about the title of the poem "Invitation." In what way is a book an invitation? Write a response in your Learner's Notebook.

LITERATURE GROUPS Meet with two or three other students who have also read these poems. Choose two or three images from the poem "To Young Readers." How do these images help the writer get across the message of the poem?

Vo•cab•u•lary

flax (flaks) a plant whose stems are used to produce pale yellow fiber that is woven into linen

REAL SPIDER SUPERPOWERS

Reported by Cameron Walker
and written by Sarah Ives

**Read to discover how spiders can outjump, outspin, and
generally outpower the superhero!**

Spider-Man appeared in movie theaters to fight villains
with his many superpowers—but real spiders have some tricks of
their own.

Real spiders may not be able to fight Doc Ock, the criminal
in *Spider-Man 2*, but some spiders *can* jump as much as 50 times
their body length.

U.S. long jumper Mike Powell holds the world's record with
a jump of 29 feet, 4.5 inches (8.95 meters). Powell is 6 feet,
2 inches (1.9 meters) tall. If he had a spider's jumping ability,

he might be able to leap 300 feet (90 meters). That would definitely bring him the gold medal in the Olympics!

Spiders jump to catch insects. "They hunt down prey, and then they'll pounce on it," said Andrew Martin, from the University of Applied Sciences in Germany.

But that's not all spiders can do. In the movies, Spider-Man walks up buildings. Some real spiders can also walk upside down on smooth surfaces.

Some spiders' feet are covered with tiny hairs. These hairs give spiders the strength to hold 170 times their body weight before coming unstuck. That would be the same as Spider-Man carrying 170 people from danger while clinging to a building with his fingers and toes, Martin said.

Scientists hope that they can use the secret of spiders' stickiness to make better sticky notes, gloves for soccer goalies, and even boots for astronauts.

Spiders can also spin as many as seven different kinds of silk. Some of the silk is so strong that it rivals the strength of steel! With skills like that, spiders could give Superman, the Man of Steel, a run for his money!

Spiders use the silk for many different purposes, like catching insects in webs, traveling from place to place, parachuting, forming egg sacs, and wrapping up prey.

According to Todd Blackledge of the University of California, Riverside, the first *Spider-Man* movie had some realistic webs. "They had such a great variety of webs," he said. "Somebody had really done their homework." ❶

❶ **Reviewing**
What "super-powers" do real spiders have?

Spider Facts

- There are more than 37,000 described spider species in the world, but only about 25 are thought to have <u>venom</u> that can affect people.

- The largest known spider is the Goliath birdeater tarantula. This South American spider can be as big as a dinner plate. The spider has even snatched birds from their nests!

- The smallest known spider is the mygalomorph (MIG-uh-low-morf) spider from Borneo. Its body is the size of a pinhead.

- Most spiders have eight eyes. But some don't have any eyes, and others can have as many as 12.

- A spider eats about 2,000 insects a year.

- Some people eat spiders. In the South Pacific, some people say spiders taste nutty and sticky like peanut butter. ○

Answering the BIG Question

As you do the following activities, consider the Big Question:
Why do we read?

WRITE TO LEARN Think about the author's purpose in writing this article. Then, write a brief entry in your Learner's Notebook about your reason for reading the article.

LITERATURE GROUPS With a small group of students who have also read this selection, list or describe the types of spiders you have seen. What information in the article surprised you the most?

Vo·cab·u·lary

venom (VEN um) a poison

BLUES FOR BOB E. BROWN

by T. Ernesto Bethancourt

Can Roberto Moreno, a. k. a. Bob E. Brown, make it as a blues singer?

Upper West Side, New York, New York

I was just getting home from my after-school delivery job at the Big Apple Market. It was about eight-thirty. I heard Mama and Papa going at it right through our apartment door. I stood outside in the hall of our second-floor walkup and tried to make out what was going on inside. **1**

1 Setting a Purpose for Reading
What do you expect to get out of reading this story?

No sense in walking into an argument unless you already know whose side you're supposed to be on. That's the trouble when you're the last kid left at home. They always want you to take sides. Ever since my older brother, Lou, left to join the Navy, it's been this way. My married sister, Margie, lives in Queens now. She's too far from West Eighty-eighth Street in Manhattan, where we live, for Mama to get her involved in her hassles with Papa.

"I don't care!" I heard Papa say. "I won't have him in my house."

"But Juanillo," I heard Mama counter, "he's your own father. Your flesh and blood . . ."

I knew Mama was trying the soft approach with Papa. When she's really pleased with him or wants something, she calls him Juanillo. Any other time, it's plain old Jack. But actually, my father's name *is* Juan—meaning "John"—and *Juanillo* means "Johnny" or "Johnny-boy."

All us kids have traditional Latino names, too. My brother Lou is really Luis Alfredo, my sister Margie is Margarita Dolores, and I'm Roberto Ernesto, although everyone calls me Bobby. I couldn't imagine anyone calling me by my middle name. Or, worse yet, *Ernie!*

My dad speaks some Spanish; so does my mom. But us kids only know a few words—me least of all, being the youngest. To give you an idea how little, I almost failed Spanish in my junior year at Brandeis High School.

The hassle was still going on inside the apartment. "My mind's made up, Helen," I heard Papa say. "If he's so interested in seeing his grandchildren after all these years, that's tough. I want nothing to do with him."

Now I knew what was going on. We had heard from my grandfather. I didn't even know he was still alive. My dad never talks about him. Seeing as how my parents' fight wasn't about me, I put my key in the door and went inside.

The hall door opens right into the kitchen of our apartment. Then comes the living room and two bedrooms. But most of the time if we aren't watching TV in the living room, most of our family life is in the kitchen.

Mama was seated at the table with her ever-present cup of Café Bustelo coffee with milk. Papa, still wearing his Transit Authority uniform, was having one of his two daily bottles of Schaefer beer. I kissed Mama and got a hug from Papa. "Hi, guys," I said. "What's happening?" As if I didn't know.

"Nothing—nothing at all, Bobby," Papa said.

"Pretty loud nothing," I said. "I heard you two down the hall."

"Oh, *that*," my dad said with a wave of a hand. "Just between your mama and me. A family matter."

"Jack!" said Mama. "You mean you aren't going to mention it?"

"Mention what?" I said, still not letting on.

My dad shook his head in a funny mix of disgust and dismay. "You might as well know, Bobby. Your grandfather has decided he's still part of our family. After all these years. We got a letter from him today."

"Grandpa's here in New York? Last time I heard you mention him, he was in California."

"He's still out there," Mama said. "But his letter says he's coming here this week. He says he wants to see us—*all* of us." Mama looked pointedly at Papa, who looked away.

"How did he even know where to find us?" I asked.

"It was your brother, Lou. He's stationed in Oakland now—"

"I know, but—?"

"Let me finish," put in Papa. "Your brother took it upon himself to track the old man down. He had some family records of my mother's that *someone* gave him." Papa looked angrily across the table at Mama. "So Lou found him—a man he'd never seen in his life—a man who didn't even come to his son's wedding."

"We know, Juanillo," Mama said softly.

"Then why should you care about a man you've never met?" my dad demanded of my mom.

"Because no matter what you say, he's your father. Yes, I know. He left when you were ten years old. But that was thirty-five years ago, Juanillo. In a way, you don't know him, either."

"I know all I need to know. My mother told me, God rest her soul."

I could see they were going to be at this for a while. I opened the fridge and took out a frozen dinner and popped it into the microwave. Then I walked down the hall to my bedroom.

I took my guitar off the chair and sat down to practice. I had an audition on Saturday night, downtown in the SoHo section of town.

I started with some simple blues changes and scales. That's my thing: traditional blues and jazz. No amplifiers—just straight acoustic. I was really getting into my solo on "Beale Street Mama" when I heard the microwave beeping.

When I came into the kitchen, Mama and Papa weren't quite so upset. Papa looked at me and said, "Well, what about it, Bobby? Do you want to meet the old man?"

"We decided it's up to you kids," Mama said. "Your father has his mind made up. He won't see your grandpa. But if you want to meet him, that's okay with us."

"What does Margie say?" I asked.

"I'm going to call her in a little while and ask."

"That's not the point," my dad said. "It's what *you* say about meeting him."

I looked at both my parents. Here I was, on the hook again. If I said yes, probably Papa would feel I was letting him down. If I said no, Mama would think I was cold. After all, I see *her* father and mother every month when they come in from Long Island. And we always have Thanksgiving dinner at their place in Oceanside. Now what was I going to say? They were looking at me, expecting some answer.

"Can I think about it?" I asked.

"Sure, honey," Mama said, ignoring Papa's look. "Take your time. He won't be coming to town until next Monday."

I took my TV dinner out of the microwave and brought it to my room. While it was cooling, I put on an old album of blues artists that I had found in a secondhand store downtown. It was made in the 1960s. The record company doesn't even exist anymore. But there sure was some good stuff on it. That record was where I learned "Beale Street Mama" from.

The guy who played and sang it was terrific. His name was Ivan Dark. I tried to find out more about him, but it seemed like this was the only recording the guy ever made. Too bad. They didn't even have a picture of him on the album cover. All it said about him was he came from New York.

But I kind of liked the idea. Almost all the great acoustic blues players came from down South, or from the South Side of Chicago. But here was a New York blues man. I had played his album track so many times, it was old and scratchy.

I ate my Budget Gourmet sirloin tips while I listened to Ivan Dark. Then I practiced until ten o'clock and went to bed. I had a full day of pedaling the delivery cart for Big Apple the next day—Saturday. And eleven-thirty that night, at Mary's Grill in SoHo, was my live audition.

Saturday at ten, I checked myself out in the bathroom mirror. I was wearing my all-black outfit: suit, shirt, tie, and shades. I debated with myself whether I should wear the black <u>fedora</u> hat. Then I decided I'd look too much like one of the Blues Brothers.

Vo•cab•u•lary

fedora (fih DOR uh) a soft, felt-brimmed hat with a crease along the crown

But I did want to look older than eighteen. My brother Lou is lucky that way. He was fifteen when he grew a moustache. I could get away with shaving twice a week. I think it's because Lou is like my dad: dark curly hair, medium complexion and build. Papa has always had a moustache, far as I can remember.

To look at me, you wouldn't think we were related. I'm tall and thin, with straight, light brown hair and hazel eyes. I took a lot of heat from kids in school about that. "Some Puerto Rican *you* are," they'd say. Called me *huero,* and a lot of other names not too choice. A lot of them just couldn't get next to a guy named Roberto Moreno who looks like I do. Mama says there's blondes on her side of the family. Maybe that's where I get my looks.

I looked at myself in the mirror and shrugged. "You are who you are, man," I told my reflection.

Then I went to my room and packed up my guitar. It's an old Gibson arch-top acoustic. The <u>pawn shop</u> guy I bought it from said it was made in the 1930s. I can believe it. But man, does that ax have a tone—a full bass and a treble that could cut glass. Just right for blues.

Mama and Papa were watching the ten o'clock news on Channel 5 as I left. We did the usual going-out-late stuff. *Yeah, I'll be careful, Mama. Papa, I know it's dangerous out there. I'll walk near the curb and away from dark doorways. Yeah, Mama, I'll call if I'm going to be late . . . .* I finally got out the door. Jeez, you'd think I was still a kid!

I hailed a cab at Amsterdam and Seventy-ninth Street. I'd been saving my tips so I could cab it both ways. You get on the subway at a late hour, and you're just asking for it. And if you're wearing a suit and carrying an instrument—well, you might as well wear a sign saying "Take me."

Mary's was in full cry when I got there. It had started out years ago as a neighborhood place that served lunches and drinks

---

Vo·cab·u·lary

pawn shop (PAWN shop) a place where money is lent in exchange for personal property

to the factory workers. But now all the factory lofts are full of artists and sculptors. The little luncheonettes and neighborhood bars changed with the times. Now they got sidewalk tables and hanging plants inside, and they serve fancy food.

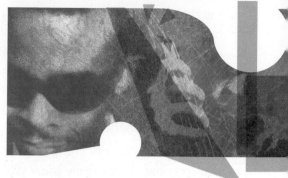

Mary's is a little different, though. They kept the old, crummy plastic-covered booths and the big, long bar. About all they changed was, they put in a little stage and a sound system. And behind the bar, they got a bunch of autographed pictures of jazz and blues musicians who played there. Some names you might know, if you're into my kind of music.

Brutus, the guy at the door, knew me and passed me in without checking any I.D. Just as well. I was using Lou's old driver's license. He gave it to me when he went into the Navy.

The place was heavy with smoke and the smell of stale beer. It's one of the few places in SoHo where they don't put the cigarette smokers in some kind of sinner's jail room. But by the late hours, the air gets so you can chew each lungful before you inhale it.

The trio onstage was tearing up a jazz number I recognized— an old Dave Brubeck tune called "Take Five," on account of it's in 5/4 time. It's the house policy at Mary's that they don't play anything there newer than bebop. I spotted Mary behind the bar, right away.

She's hard to miss. Five four and easily two hundred pounds, with a flaming red wig that was probably new when the Beatles were big. She gave me a huge grin and waved me over. "Bob E. Brown, you rascal!" she hollered over the trio and the crowd noise. "I was wondering if you was gonna show. You're on in fifteen minutes."

Maybe I ought to explain about that Bob E. Brown. See, when I decided to be a blues man, Roberto Moreno didn't sound right for that line of work. I was already Bobby, and Moreno means brown in Spanish. And because there's already a rock singer named Bobby Brown, I came up with Bob E. Brown—the "E" being for Ernesto. It sounds the same as Bobby. It's just spelled different. It's no sin or anything to change your name. After all, Muddy Waters's real name was McKinley Morganfield. **❷**

> **❷ Setting a Purpose for Reading**
> Has your purpose for reading this story remained the same?

I took the empty stool at the end of the long bar. Mary drew me a Coke with a piece of lime in it. "Try and act like it's a Cuba Libre, rascal," Mary said. "Don't want to give the customers the wrong idea." Mary knew I was underage, and I don't drink, anyway. But she's in the business of selling drinks.

She leaned across the bar, and a lot of Mary rested on the hardwood. "Best you tune up in the kitchen, rascal," she said. "The group will want the downstairs dressing room when they get off. You ready?"

"As I'll ever get." I didn't want to admit I felt shaky. Sure, I had played at neighborhood places and at assemblies in school. But this was different. This was *professional*.

Even when I had performed for Mary, it was in the daytime. And Mary's easy to be with and play for. It's like she's everyone's mama. I took a quick sip of my drink, then went into the kitchen to tune up.

When I came out, the trio was just finishing up. There was a light dusting of applause. It seemed like the crowd was more interested in each other than in what was happening onstage. Mary got up and announced, "Let's have a nice hand for the Milt Lewis Trio, folks." A little more clapping was all that got her.

"Tonight," Mary went on, "we have a special treat for you. A young man who's making his first appearance here at Mary's, the home of good jazz and blues. Please welcome a new generation blues man—Bob E. Brown!"

I swallowed a lump in my throat the size of a baseball and got onstage to some indifferent applause. "Go get 'em, rascal," Mary whispered to me. I adjusted the mike in front of the chair on the stage—I work sitting down—and went right into a Bessie Smith tune, "Gimme a Pig's Foot."

Halfway through, I realized I was making as much impression as a snowball on a brick wall. I started to feel dribbles of sweat creep down my back. *What am I doing here?* I thought. *I must have been crazy to try this!* I finished the chorus and went into my vocal.

That was when it happened. Something clicked in my mind. If these people didn't want to listen, that was okay. What I was doing was between me and my guitar. If they liked it—swell. If they didn't, I still had my music.

I threw back my head, not caring and sang, "Gimme a pig's foot and a bottle of beer. Send me gate, 'cause I don't care . . .." The damnedest thing happened. The house got quieter. Every now and then, when I looked up from the finger board of my ax, I could see heads turning and faces looking at me. The sweat on my back and on the palms of my hands started to dry out.

When I got to the last line, "Slay me 'cause I'm in my sin . . . .," they began clapping. They applauded all the way through the last four bars I played solo to finish the tune. I couldn't believe it. They liked me!

The next two tunes were a blur in my mind. Oh, I know what songs I did. I just don't remember paying attention to *how* I did them. All the hours and years of practice took over. I didn't watch my hands, like I usually do. I watched the faces of those people watching me. I sang *to* them, not at them. ❸

❸ **Reviewing**
How did Bob E. Brown gain the crowd's applause?

The great blues man, Josh White, said that he didn't sing songs, he told stories. And every song is a story. I told those folks my story—but in the words of the blues I sang.

I glanced over and saw Mary. She had come out from behind the bar and was standing only a few feet away. She was smiling like it would bust her face. She waved and put one index finger across the tip of the other to form a letter T. That meant it was time for me to do my last number. I finished the tune I was playing, and the house really came apart.

For the first time, I spoke directly to the crowd. "Thank you very much," I said, my voice a lightly shaky. "I'd like to finish up with a tune I learned from a recording by a New York blues man, Ivan Dark. It's called 'Beale Street Mama.'"

I went into the intro, and they were already clapping. I played the first chorus and went into the vocal: "'Beale Street Mama, won't you come on home . . . .'" As I did, I was startled by the sound of the upright bass from behind me. I almost missed a chord change. Out of the corner of my eye, I saw that the Milt Lewis Trio had come onstage behind me.

Then we really started to cook. Milt Lewis plays alto sax, and with the bass and a drummer added, we did I don't know how many choruses. I dropped into rhythm playing while everyone took his solo, then we all finished together.

In my entire life, I never felt anything like that. Nothing compared. Not even Angela Ruiz in the hall outside her folks' apartment. When we played the last note, there was a moment of silence, like the crowd wanted to make sure we were finished. Then the place blew up with clapping, hollers, and whistles.

Suddenly, Mary was at my side. "Let's hear it for Bob E. Brown!" she shouted over the din.

"Let's hear more!" somebody in the house hollered. "Yeah, more!"

another voice said.

"We got all night, folks," Mary said. She put a huge meaty arm around my waist. "We gotta let this rascal get some rest. Don't worry. He'll be back . . . Bob E. Brown, ladies and gentlemen. Remember that name!"

I got offstage on a cloud. As Mary led the way to the bar, people applauded as I went by. Some of them reached out and shook my hand. Lots of them said nice things as I went by.

Back at the bar, Mary drew a Coke with lime and set it in front of me. "Well, rascal, seems like you got the stuff," she said. "And if you want a gig, you got one here. Milt and the guys start a road tour in two more weeks.

"But I like the sound you made together. Can you pick up a trio to work with?"

I almost fell off the bar stool. "I don't know any other musicians," I admitted, my face feeling warm.

Mary frowned. "Bet you don't have a union card, either," she said. I shook my head. Then she smiled that five-hundred-watt grin. "Then you gotta get busy, rascal. You get your little butt up to the union hall. Tell them you got a contract here. They can call me to check it out.

"Pay them the fee. You'll have your card fast enough, if I know that local. And believe me, I know that local. You start in two weeks. I'll book a trio to back you."

It wasn't until I was in a cab headed home after one more show that Mary's words sank in. A fee? How much did it cost to join the musicians' union, anyway? But I was too tired and too happy to think about it that night. I was somebody. I was Bob E. Brown—a real blues man!

I nearly died when I found out on Monday what the union initiation fee was. I called Local 802 and spent about twenty minutes on the phone. If I drew every cent from my savings account, I was still five hundred dollars short. Half a thousand: all the money in the world!

I put down the phone and stared at the kitchen walls. Mama

and Papa were still at work. I had thirty minutes to get over to the Big Apple Market, and I still hadn't eaten a thing. I went to the fridge and saw the note from Mama on the door.

Bobby, your grandfather called. He wants you to call him at his hotel, the Waldorf-Astoria. He's in Room 1620. The decision is yours.

I took some spiced ham from the fridge and made myself a quick sandwich. There was no Pepsi left, so I got a glass of water to wash it down with. As I ate, I thought, *So he's in town, huh? Guess I gotta make up my mind.*

But to tell the truth, all that was on my mind was that five hundred bucks. How in the name of anything was I going to raise that in two weeks? I had finally gotten a professional gig, and now I was in danger of losing it. It was driving me nuts.

More to get my mind off it than anything else, I dialed the hotel. After two rings a woman's voice said, "Waldorf-Astoria Hotel. How may we help you?" ❹

❹ Reviewing
What was on Bobby's mind when he phoned his grandfather's hotel?

I couldn't believe it. I'd only walked past the Waldorf. My grandfather was actually staying there, at one of the ritziest places in town. I gave the switchboard operator the room number. It rang for a while before anyone picked up and a man's voice said hello.

"Mr. Moreno, please," I said.

"Which Mr. Moreno?"

All of a sudden, I had to think of what my grandfather's first name was. Then it came to me: same as Papa—Juan. That's who I asked for. "Just a moment," the voice said.

"This is Juan Moreno," a new voice said.

"This is Bobby, your grandson, I think. My mother left me a note to call you."

The voice warmed. "Bobby! How are you, kid? Yeah, this is your grandpa. Where are you? When can we get together?"

"Uh—I don't know. I'm home right now, but I got to go to work in a few minutes."

"I thought you were still in school, kid."

"I am. I work afterward."

"Until when?"

"Eight o'clock."

"Good enough. We'll have dinner. Get a cab. I'll leave money with the doorman. You know where I am?"

"The Waldorf-Astoria?"

"That's right. But I'm in the Waldorf *Towers*. That's the side entrance, not the Park Avenue one. Tell the cabbie; he'll know. See you about eight-thirty, okay?"

"I ought to clean up and change, right?"

"Okay, then. Nine o'clock. I'll be waiting, Bobby."

When I arrived at the hotel, I was wearing the same outfit I did at the Mary's audition, but with a white tie. I figured if I was going to have dinner at a place like this, I'd need one.

My grandfather had taken care of business. The doorman had money for my cab and even tipped the driver for me. And when he showed me into the lobby and what elevator to take, he called me Mister Moreno! I'd been having quite a different kind of life, lately. First I was Bob E. Brown, the blues man. Now I was *Mister Moreno*.

I rang the bell at my grandfather's door, and a guy about twenty opened it. He was my size and build, with dark hair and eyes. He was wearing a designer shirt and slacks, with a pair of shoes that would cost me a month's pay at the Big Apple. "Come in," the guy said, extending a hand for me to shake. "You must be Bobby. I'm your Uncle Jim."

It wasn't a hotel room he led me into. It was an apartment like I never had seen, even in a movie. "Dad!" my "Uncle Jim" called out. "Bobby's here."

A man came out of the next room, and I went into shock. If someone had given me a magic mirror to show me what I'd look like in fifty-five years, here I was!

He had a full head of straight white hair. He was thin and

over six feet tall and had a deep suntan that made his hair look silver. His eyes were the same color as mine, too. He was wearing a lightweight suit that screamed money, and a conservative tie.

As he extended his arms to give me an *abrazo*, I saw, from beneath the white cuff of his shirt, the glint of a gold Rolex. This was my grandpa?

He threw a bear hug around me, then stepped back and held me at arm's length. "So you're Bobby, huh?" he said. "I'd have known you anywhere, kid. Same as I'd know myself.

"Here, sit down," he said, waving me to a chair. "You want something to drink? Jimmy, get Bobby what he wants," he told my "uncle." "You've already met Jimmy, right?"

I just nodded. I was numb. Finally, I said, "He's my uncle?"

My grandpa laughed. "Yeah, he is. Not much older than you, though." He looked at me and laughed again. "I've been married a few times since your grandma, kid. Jimmy's from the latest edition. What can he give you?"

"A Coke would be fine, sir."

"Sir? What is that crap? Call me Grandpa. I kind of like it." Jimmy came over and handed me the soda. I thanked him.

"What about I leave you two alone, Dad?" Jimmy asked. "I have to get downtown, anyway."

"Have a good time, Jimmy," Grandpa said. "You got enough money?"

"I'm fine, Dad."

"And don't forget. If they won't let you tape the group, I want a full report on what you think."

Jimmy had put on a leather jacket from a closet near the door. I know guys on West Eighty-eighth that would kill for one like it. "Come on, Dad," he said. "If I don't know the business by now…"

"How do you run it when I step down?" Grandpa finished. "Okay, boy. Have a good time."

Jimmy left and Grandpa focused in on me. He sat down on the sofa facing my chair and leaned forward. "But tell me about yourself, kid," he said, "and about your family. I know a lot from your brother, Lou. Your sister isn't going to see me. And your mom has to side with your father. That I can understand. You're the only family I got here that's talking to me, it seems."

I thought I saw a far-off look of sadness in the old man's eyes. I don't know why, but I started to talk. He was a good listener. He didn't break in, and I could tell from the expression on his face that he was interested in what I had to say.

I told him everything: my dreams, the gig at Mary's coming up, my feeling about being a blues man. All except the money for the musicians' union. I could see the old man was rich, but I didn't want him to think that that was why I had come to see him.

When I'd finished talking, he went over to the bar in the corner and poured himself a tall glass of tonic water with ice. He saw me watching him and smiled. "I don't drink anymore," he said. "Not my idea. It's the doctors. I stopped smoking, drinking, and eating Caribbean cooking. I may not live a long time," he said, taking a sip of the tonic water, "but it sure as hell will *feel* like it." He set the glass down by the bar. "Stay here," he said. "I'll be right back." He went into the other room.

I sat there trying to digest all that had happened. My grandpa was something else. He had to be almost seventy—sixty-five at the youngest. Yet he was so *alive*. Not like my mama's dad, who really looks tired.

And what really knocked me out was that this guy didn't have a trace of an accent. My other grandpa talks like Ricky Ricardo on *I Love Lucy*. He didn't even have a New York accent like Mama and Papa. He came back into the room with a flat-top acoustic guitar, and I nearly fell off the chair.

It wasn't nylon strung, either. It was a Martin, model D-28. I knew it right away. That's how come I'd bought the Gibson. I couldn't afford one like this. He held it out to me and said, "It's already in tune, kid."

He went over to the bar and brought me one of the stools. "No straight-back chairs here," he said. "This will have to do. Okay, play for me."

"Play what?"

"Whatever you think I'd like best. Or better yet, what *you* like best. Please yourself enough, you'll please your audience." He sat down on the couch.

I played "Beale Street Mama," naturally. I'd already told him how well it had gone down when I played at Mary's. When I finished, he reached inside his back pocket and took out a hankie that looked like it was silk. He blew his nose like a trumpet playing an A natural. He gave me a look that had no name on it and said, "You got the stuff, kid."

"That's what Mary said," I replied.

"She would. Mary and me go back thirty-five years. When her husband was still alive and ran the Jazz Stop on Hudson Street."

"How do you know Mary?"

"Give me the guitar, kid," he said. I handed the Martin over. And he played. "Beale Street Mama."

A creepy feeling came over me. Every last lick I had practiced for hours just flowed from under his fingers. Then he sang the first chorus. The voice was deeper and darker, but the phrasing was there. I started to feel like I was in the middle of a *Twilight Zone*.

When he finished, I couldn't say a word. I just looked at him. My other grandpa is a retired garment worker. His idea of music runs to old-time stuff like you hear in the black-and-white musicals on Televisa, the Spanish-language network on UHF.

"You know the record, too!" I finally got out.

"Kid, I *made* the record," Grandpa said. "If your Spanish was better, you could have figured that out. Moreno doesn't mean brown, like you think. It means *dark*. In Russian, Juan is *Ivan*. That's how I became Ivan Dark. Who ever heard of a blues man from New York named Juan Moreno?"

"But how come you never made any more records?"

"I did. Lots of them. Just not as Ivan Dark. Got into Latino jazz. It's where I really belonged to begin with."

"But you were—are so good."

"Doesn't matter, Bobby. Sure I was good. I learned from the best. They were still alive in the late fifties and early sixties. Josh White, the Reverend Gray Davis, Mississippi John Hurt, Muddy Waters. I worked with all of them and learned by watching and listening.

"But good isn't great. And those men were great. There were other young guys who hung around and played blues. They're all gone, most of them.

"A guy I knew in nineteen fifty-seven is still at it. His name's Dave Van Ronk. He had his thirty-year anniversary in the music business this weekend. That's part of what brought me to town. They had a big blowout at the Village Gate. I was there on Sunday."

"But why did you stop playing blues?" I insisted.

"I finally figured it out, Bobby. Even though my folks learned their English from Black people—that's the neighborhoods we lived in after they came here from San Juan, and that's the first 'American' music I heard—it's not our culture.

"I could play rings around lots of Black kids my age. That didn't matter. I wasn't accepted, really.

"Dave Van Ronk is a white man from Astoria, Queens. I don't know if Dave was too dumb or too stubborn to quit. But I heard him last night. And he's a blues man down to his toenails."

"And so you quit?"

"I never quit!" said the old man, sitting up straight. "I went into my Latino roots. I found a way to meld Latino and jazz music. And I did well. I've got a club in Oakland, my own record label, and I do just fine."

"I'm sorry," I said. "I didn't mean to make you mad, Grandpa." But I knew I had said the wrong thing. I got up. "Well, I guess I have to go now."

"Why? We didn't even have dinner. I can call room service. Look, kid. I don't want to lose touch with you. We hardly started to know each other."

I came out and said what was on my mind. "Look, Grandpa. Maybe it was different when you were coming up. But there's lots of kids of all backgrounds who play blues, jazz, even soul. **5**

"That's the great thing about music. It cuts across all lines today. The Milt Lewis Trio is Black; they never said anything but how much they liked what I did. Mary is Black, and she's gonna give me a job at her club. And are you gonna tell me that Joe Cocker, a white Englishman, has no soul?

5 Reviewing How has the blues scene changed since Ivan's day?

"What brings us all together is the music. And it don't matter where you come from or where you're at. You're Juan Moreno. I'm gonna be Bob E. Brown."

The old man stood up and smiled. "Maybe your Uncle Jimmy is right, kid," he said. "It's time for me to step down. Us old guys think we know it all. Maybe we can learn a lot from you kids. If we're smart enough to listen. I wish you well."

I got up and headed for the door. "It's getting late, Grandpa,"

I said. "And I got school tomorrow."

"I'll give you cab fare," he said.

"That's okay," I replied. "The subway's still running." I knew I was taking a chance wearing a suit, but I didn't want to ask the old man for anything more.

"You sure?" he asked.

"You already gave me 'Beale Street Mama,'" I answered. "Thanks, *abuelo*." I took an *abrazo* from him and left.

I get regular letters from him now. I write when I can. The first letter I wrote was a thank-you. He got in touch with Mary the next day. He also paid my whole initiation fee to Local 802. When I got my union card, it was already made out. In the space that reads "Member's Name" it said Roberto Moreno. But there's another space on the card for the name you play under: your stage name. In that space, Grandpa had had the clerk put in *Ivan Dark II*.

I was really grateful for what Grandpa did. And I love the old man for it. But to hell with that *Ivan Dark II*. I'm Bob E. Brown, and I'll show the world I am. **6** ◯

6 Reviewing
How has Roberto changed since the beginning of the story?

Answering the BIG Question

As you do the following activities, consider the Big Question:
Why do we read?

WRITE TO LEARN Bob E. Brown discovers what makes his heart sing. Make a brief entry in your Learner's Notebook about what makes your heart sing. How can you take the first step in finding out who you are?

LITERATURE GROUPS Get together with two or three others who have also read this story. Discuss the role Bob E. Brown's grandfather played in his career. Do you think Bob E. Brown would have succeeded without his grandfather's help?

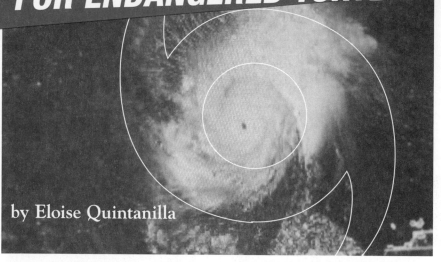

HURRICANE EMILY BAD NEWS FOR ENDANGERED TURTLES

by Eloise Quintanilla

Read to discover how Hurricane Emily affected turtles on the beaches in Mexico.

Storm sweeps away 84,000 eggs on Mexican beach ❶

❶ Previewing
What do the photos and the subhead tell you?

AKUMAL, Mexico — When Hurricane Emily tore through the <u>Yucatan Peninsula</u> on July 17, 2005, it destroyed nearly all the eggs that had been laid that season by endangered sea turtles on the white sand beach of Xcacel.

On the Gulf Coast of Mexico about 60 miles south of Cancun, the stretch of beach near Akumal is one of the most

---

Vo·cab·u·lary

Yucatan Peninsula (YOO kah tahn puh NIN suh luh) stretch of land that extends into the Gulf of Mexico

important nesting grounds in Mexico for green and loggerhead sea turtles. Alejandro Arenas Martinez, director of the Xcacel sea turtle conservation program, said that more than 84,000 eggs were swept away.

"In all of the 15 years I have been working here, a hurricane has never hit so hard, so early in the season," he said. The effect of the loss of the eggs will be felt several years down the line, he said, when this summer's generation was set to lay their own eggs. Arenas said that an average of 80 percent of the eggs, or 67,000, would have hatched.

A sea turtle off the coast of Mexico

Looking down at the lone surviving nest—of more than 700—Arenas sighs. "These eggs were laid on July 16, one day before the hurricane hit. Except for this one nest, every egg laid after May 17 was lost." ○

Answering the BIG Question

As you do the following activities, consider the Big Question:
Why do we read?

WRITE TO LEARN Think about the author's purpose in writing this article. In your Learner's Notebook, jot down what you learned about endangered sea turtles in Mexico.

PARTNER TALK Meet with a partner who has also read this selection. Discuss how the eggs were lost. Could this have been prevented?

NAKED ANIMALS

by David George Gordon

Read to discover how some animals have adapted to their environments.

Without fur or hair, most mammals would be pretty uncomfortable. That's because a furry covering shields mammals' bodies from the weather, keeping them warm and dry—sort of like your clothes do for you.

Of the 5,000 kinds of wild mammals, only a few are nearly hairless. These creatures developed other ways to thrive comfortably.

Furless Pets ❶

A few animals, such as the sphynx cat and the Mexican hairless dog, are practically hairless because people bred them that way.

They're bred as pets.

A sphynx generally feels like <u>suede</u> to the touch. Some sphynxes have very fine, hard-to-see body hair. They feel like warm, fresh peaches!

> **❶ Previewing**
> What do the subheads on this page and the next page tell you?

Vo•cab•u•lary

suede (swayd) soft leather with a velvet-like feel

Many Animals Thrive in Their Near-Nakedness.

Elephants, rhinos, and hippos don't have fur. They all live in hot places, where the trick is to keep cool. Being practically hairless is one way these animals deal with the heat. They use mud, dust, and water to protect their skin from sunburn.

Whales spend all of their time underwater. Their body fat keeps them warm, so they don't need fur coats. Naked mole rats live entirely underground, where the temperature stays warm year-round. No need for hair there!

Hair has a special importance for some animals. If it's long and colorful, or short and cropped in different shapes, it can attract lots of attention from the opposite sex. Think about that the next time you see a male lion's mane at the zoo or a teenager with a spiked Mohawk hairstyle at the mall!

Are We Naked?

Some people call humans "naked apes." That's not entirely accurate, though. An adult human's body is covered with about five million hairs—the same number that an adult gorilla has. However, human hair is generally shorter and thinner than gorilla hair. You may have to look closely to see the hairs on most of your body. **2** ○

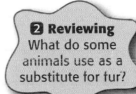

2 Reviewing
What do some animals use as a substitute for fur?

Answering the BIG Question

As you do the following activities, consider the Big Question:
Why do we read?

WRITE TO LEARN Think about the author's purpose in writing this article. Then, write a brief entry in your Learner's Notebook about your reason for reading the article.

LITERATURE GROUPS Join two or three other students who have read "Naked Animals." Discuss your reaction to hairless animals, particularly pets.

ANIMAL HOUSE

by Heather Herman

Should circuses be allowed to include animals in their shows?

Fifteen-year-old Heather Herman is fighting to free animals from performing in circuses and parades. She just might win. ❶

People have come up to me and said, "The circus is a Denver tradition:"—there's a neighborhood here named for

❶ Previewing
What do you expect to learn about circus animals?

P.T. Barnum—"how can you try to stop the circus?" Or, "You're a kid, you're supposed to love the circus!" But this isn't about the circus; it's about the animals. There are so many people in our generation who believe that using wild animals for entertainment is just wrong. If we do something about this now, watching elephants, tigers, and other animals perform won't be a tradition by the time we grow up. We'll have a new tradition, our own tradition.

I've been learning and thinking about animals since I was in fourth grade, when my dad showed me some <u>brochures</u> about animal cruelty that he'd gotten from a co-worker. I looked at them and thought, *This is so awful. I want to do something to help.* Over the years I wrote letters to the local newspaper and did some research on the Web to find organizations that would send me information, like the Humane Society, but somehow I didn't feel I was making a real difference. I was especially upset by what was going on in circuses. I'd always thought animals in the circus were just like pets performing tricks. I didn't realize you had to train them with physical force and that they travel in really small cages. The trainers often do things that you would never do to your dog or cat—you wouldn't strike your puppy with a whip if he didn't do what you asked! Or leave your cat in a cage so tiny she couldn't even turn around. I couldn't believe this was happening and that nothing was being done about it.

I asked different groups what I should do when the circus came to town. They told me to go out and protest. I thought, *Well, that doesn't help the animals.*

So, two years ago, when I was thirteen, I began to wonder about trying to make a change. At first, people didn't take me seriously—they just thought, *Oh, there goes Heather again.* In the past, I had started crazy little neighborhood-club things—a church newspaper, volunteer work here and there—and never really followed through on any of them. But when I learned

---

Vo•cab•u•lary

brochures (broh SHOORZ) small booklets containing information about a product or particular interest

that the city of Boulder, Colorado, had already outlawed animal circuses, I thought it'd be great to do something like that in Denver. (There are at least 20 circuses touring the country that don't feature animal acts.)

I got in touch with a group called the Rocky Mountain Animal Defense (RMAD) to find out how I could get Denver to ban animal circuses too. I learned that I needed to call the city's Election Commission, which is in charge of putting <u>initiatives</u> on the ballot for a citywide vote.

I had no idea how to get a law passed, and neither did my parents. From the commission office I found out I had to file a Citizen's <u>Petition</u> and get 5,000 signatures from registered Denver voters before the initiative could be placed on a ballot. At the time, it seemed so complicated and nearly impossible. Luckily, RMAD took me seriously and they offered to help organize support. In addition, I formed my own organization, Youth Opposed to Animal Acts, to get people interested in the issue. My friends and I spent weekends standing outside grocery stores collecting signatures. We went to the local fair and collected; we went to school sporting events; we went door-to-door. (We always had an adult with us because the law says you have to be eighteen to gather signatures.) Some people were pretty rude, and would say, "What do you want, money?" before practically closing the door in our faces.

A lot of people said, "Wow, you are really young." Or, sometimes, "You can't do this, it's too complicated." But it's not; it's just that most of us don't pay attention to how the system works. It's our right to petition the government, to assemble publicly, to speak freely. We *can* make a difference! It's amazing to me that I've been a part of this, that I stuck to the commitment.

At the end of the summer, after we had collected a little

Vo•cab•u•lary

initiatives (ih NISH uh tivz) proposals for new laws
petition (puh TIH shun) a written demand, with signatures, for legal action

Heather Herman, founder of Youth Opposed to Animal Acts, gets out the vote.

more than 5,000 signatures, the commission dropped the bomb on us: We needed 3,000 more! Only about 2,000 of ours were valid. School was starting and I had marching band practice after class, so there wasn't much time to collect signatures. My friends and I couldn't believe that we'd spent all summer on something that was falling apart. Some wondered if it was worth following through.

But I couldn't give up. Even though I was pretty tired and crabby, I thought about those pictures of elephants with cuts through their skin, and tigers with their claws removed. I decided to send letters to national animal groups requesting donations so that we could hire signature collectors. We got nine national organizations to help out, plus our parents and some of their friends, with our weekend supermarket posts.

On November 5, 2003, we turned in our petition to ban animal acts in circuses performing in Denver, with more than 10,000 signatures! We celebrated at a vegetarian restaurant—

it was an incredible day. Then in January, I spoke at a public hearing before the Denver City Council. I spoke for six minutes— I've never been so nervous—and the story made the front page of the *Rocky Mountain News*. That's when all the TV and radio stations started to call and it turned into a big national story.

The vote comes up this month,[1] and I'm anxious to see the outcome. Maybe someday I will take this a step further and help people in other cities get a similar initiative passed. It would be so amazing if the entire state of Colorado agreed to ban circuses with animals. But that's hundreds of thousands of signatures, which is a lot of hours standing in front of the grocery store! O

Answering the BIG Question

As you do the following activities, consider the Big Question: **Why do we read?**

WRITE TO LEARN Heather learned how circus animals were treated when she read a brochure on the subject. Think about how you might make a difference in your community. Write a brief entry in your Learner's Notebook.

LITERATURE GROUPS Join two or three other students who have read "Animal House." Discuss your responses to the article. How do you feel about Heather's campaign? Do you think animal acts should be banned in circuses?

. . . .

[1] Although voters defeated this proposal on August 10, 2004, it did bring great attention to the treatment of circus animals. Animal rights groups were encouraged by the level of awareness the proposal raised. They vow to continue their struggle for humane treatment of circus animals.

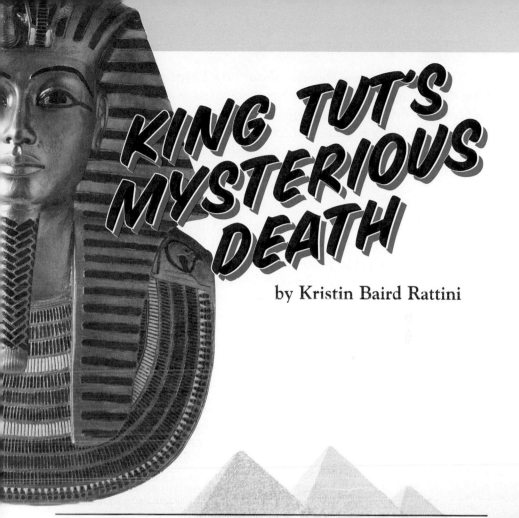

KING TUT'S MYSTERIOUS DEATH

by Kristin Baird Rattini

What caused the sudden and mysterious death of King Tut?

King Tutankhamun's army just lost a major battle. His subjects could be facing a terrible <u>plague</u>. Egypt's king probably has a lot on his mind as he goes to bed for the night. Suddenly someone leaps out of the shadows and strikes the king with a fatal blow to the back of the head. Tut's nine-year reign comes to a quick and mysterious end.

Vo•cab•u•lary

plague (playg) a disease that infects large numbers of people and kills many of those infected

That's one of many theories about how Egypt's most famous king died at age 19. The puzzle has fascinated researchers since 1922, when British archaeologist Howard Carter discovered Tut's 3,300-year-old tomb. Determined to find the answer, National Geographic Explorer-in-Residence Zahi Hawass used modern technology to put this old theory to the test.

The Investigation

"I was almost trembling when I arrived at the tomb," Hawass says. His team of experts carefully removed King Tut's mummy from its royal grave and placed it in a computed tomography (CT) scanner. The machine created detailed images of Tut's mummy, which were reconstructed on a computer. That way scientists could examine Tut from any angle without damaging him. The result? New clues in this ancient mystery! **1**

> **1 Understanding Text Structure**
> In what order does the writer describe the scientists' procedure?

First Suspect

An old x-ray of King Tut, taken in 1968, showed a bone fragment loose in the back of the mummy's skull and a possible head injury. Many investigators suspected that Tut had been fatally hit from behind. But who would gain from the pharaoh's death? Perhaps it was his close advisor Aye. Much older and more experienced than the king, Aye had great power. Was he hungry for more? After all, Aye did take over as pharaoh after Tut's death.

Second Suspect

Or maybe Tut's army commander, Horemheb, was the culprit. As Egypt's military leader, Horemheb was supposed to protect his country. But did the king need protection from him? Horemheb became pharaoh after Aye and removed all mentions of Tut from

---

Vo·cab·u·lary

archaeologist (ar kee OL uh jist) a scientist who studies ancient peoples by examining their material remains
pharaoh (FAIR oh) an ancient Egyptian ruler

public monuments. Aye and Horemheb make good suspects, but Hawass's team concludes that Tut wasn't hit from behind after all. The CT scan shows that the bone broke into fragments after Tut's death. The damage probably occurred when Tut's body was mummified or when Carter removed the mummy from its coffin.

More Clues

It's unlikely that a teenage king would have died of natural causes. So what really happened? Could Tut have died as a result of an accident? The mummy's breastbone and many of its ribs were missing. Some think Tut may have fallen in battle, or taken his chariot for a deadly joy ride. "If that were true, the CT scan would have shown damage to Tut's spine," Hawass says. "But it didn't." Could the king have been poisoned or did he catch a deadly disease? CT scans can't tell us everything, but the scientists found no evidence of long-term poisoning or illness.

A Break in the Case

The CT scan did reveal an important clue: a broken left leg. Some experts think the break happened just days before Tut died, which caused a life-threatening infection.

Others think Carter's team accidentally broke the bone. That makes this just one more theory in King Tut's unsolved death. Says Hawass: "The mystery continues." O

Answering the BIG Question

As you do the following activities, consider the Big Question: **Why do we read?**

WRITE TO LEARN Think about the author's purpose in writing this article. Then, jot down your reason for reading. What kept you interested? Write a brief entry in your Learner's Notebook.

PARTNER TALK With a partner who has also read this selection, discuss your responses to the article. Which theory do you think is the most likely explanation for King Tut's untimely death?

RIKKI-TIKKI-TAVI

by Rudyard Kipling

**Read to see what happens when a little mongoose tries to
outsmart a pair of deadly king cobras.**

his is the story of the great war that Rikki-tikki-tavi
fought single-handed, through the bathrooms of the big bungalow
in <u>Segowlee</u> cantonment.[1] Darzee, the <u>tailorbird</u>, helped him, and
Chuchundra, the <u>muskrat</u>, who never comes out into the middle

· ·

[1] In India, a cantonment was a British military "town" where servicemen and
their families lived in separate bungalows, or cottages.

Vo•cab•u•lary

Segowlee (seg OW lee) in Nepal, a center of British occupation when
this story takes place
tailorbird (TAY lur burd) a tropical bird that stitches plant fibers
together to make a nest
muskrat (MUSK rat) a large rodent that spends much time in and
around water

of the floor, but always creeps round by the wall, gave him advice; but Rikki-tikki did the real fighting. **❶**

❶ Previewing
Look at the pictures and read an occasional paragraph to see how the story will unfold.

He was a mongoose, rather like a little cat in his fur and his tail, but quite like a weasel in his head and his habits. His eyes and the end of his restless nose were pink; he could scratch himself anywhere he pleased, with any leg, front or back, that he chose to use; he could fluff up his tail till it looked like a bottle brush, and his war cry, as he <u>scuttled</u> through the long grass, was "*Rikk-tikk-tikki-tikki-tchk!*"

One day, a high summer flood washed him out of the burrow where he lived with his father and mother and carried him, kicking and clucking, down a roadside ditch. He found a little wisp of grass floating there, and clung to it till he lost his senses. When he revived, he was lying in the hot sun on the middle of a garden path, very <u>draggled</u> indeed, and a small boy was saying: "Here's a dead mongoose. Let's have a funeral."

"No," said his mother, "let's take him in and dry him. Perhaps he isn't really dead."

They took him into the house, and a big man picked him up between his finger and thumb and said he was not dead but half choked; so they wrapped him in cotton wool and warmed him, and he opened his eyes and sneezed.

"Now," said the big man (he was an Englishman who had just moved into the bungalow), "don't frighten him, and we'll see what he'll do."

It is the hardest thing in the world to frighten a mongoose, because he is eaten from nose to tail with curiosity. The motto of all the mongoose family is "Run and find out"; and Rikki-tikki was a true mongoose. He looked at the cotton wool, decided that

---

Vo•cab•u•lary

scuttled (SKUT uld) ran with short, hurried movements
draggled (DRAG uld) made wet and dirty by dragging on the ground

51

it was not good to eat, ran all round the table, sat up and put his fur in order, scratched himself, and jumped on the small boy's shoulder.

"Don't be frightened, Teddy," said his father. "That's his way of making friends."

"Ouch! He's tickling under my chin," said Teddy.

Rikki-tikki looked down between the boy's collar and neck, snuffed at his ear, and climbed down to the floor, where he sat rubbing his nose.

"Good gracious," said Teddy's mother, "and that's a wild creature! I suppose he's so tame because we've been kind to him."

"All mongooses are like that," said her husband. "If Teddy doesn't pick him up by the tail, or try to put him in a cage, he'll run in and out of the house all day long. Let's give him something to eat."

They gave him a little piece of raw meat. Rikki-tikki liked it immensely, and when it was finished he went out into the veranda and sat in the sunshine and fluffed up his fur to make it dry to the roots. Then he felt better.

"There are more things to find out about in this house," he said to himself, "than all my family could find out in all their lives. I shall certainly stay and find out." ❷

He spent all that day roaming over the house. He nearly drowned himself in the bathtubs, put his nose into the ink on a writing table, and burned it on the end of the big man's cigar, for he climbed up in the big man's lap to see how writing was done. At nightfall he ran into Teddy's nursery to watch how <u>kerosene</u> lamps were lighted, and when Teddy went to bed Rikki-tikki climbed up too; but he was a restless companion, because he had to get up and attend to every

❷ **Reviewing**
How did Rikki first come to live in the bungalow?

Vo•cab•u•lary

kerosene (KER uh seen) a liquid fuel made from petroleum

noise all through the night and find out what made it.

Teddy's mother and father came in, the last thing, to look at their boy, and Rikki-tikki was awake on the pillow. "I don't like that," said Teddy's mother; "he may bite the child."

"He'll do no such thing," said the father. "Teddy's safer with that little beast than if he had a bloodhound to watch him. If a snake came into the nursery now—"

But Teddy's mother wouldn't think of anything so awful.

Early in the morning Rikki-tikki came to early breakfast in the <u>veranda</u>, riding on Teddy's shoulder, and they gave him banana and some boiled egg; and he sat on all their laps one after the other, because every well-brought-up mongoose always hopes to be a house mongoose someday and have rooms to run about in, and Rikki-tikki's mother (she used to live in the general's house at Segowlee) had carefully told Rikki what to do if ever he came across Englishmen.

Then Rikki-tikki went out into the garden to see what was to be seen. It was a large garden, only half <u>cultivated</u>, with bushes as big as summer houses of roses, lime and orange trees, clumps

Vo•cab•u•lary

veranda (vuh RAN duh) porch
cultivated (KUL tuh vayt ud) planted

of bamboos, and thickets of high grass. Rikki-tikki licked his lips. "This is a splendid hunting ground," he said, and his tail grew bottle-brushy at the thought of it, and he scuttled up and down the garden, snuffling here and there till he heard very sorrowful voices in a thornbush.

It was Darzee, the tailorbird, and his wife. They had made a beautiful nest by pulling two big leaves together and stitching them up the edges with fibers, and had filled the hollow with cotton and downy fluff. The nest swayed to and fro, as they sat on the brim and cried.

"What is the matter?" asked Rikki-tikki.

"We are very miserable," said Darzee. "One of our babies fell out of the nest yesterday, and Nag ate him."

"H'm!" said Rikki-tikki; "that is very sad—but I am a stranger here. Who is Nag?"

Darzee and his wife only <u>cowered</u> down in the nest without answering, for from the thick grass at the foot of the bush came a low hiss—a horrid cold sound that made Rikki-tikki jump back two clear feet. Then inch by inch out of the grass rose up the head and spread hood of Nag, the big black cobra, and he was five feet long from tongue to tail. When he had lifted one-third of himself clear of the ground, he stayed balancing to and fro exactly as a dandelion tuft balances in the wind, and he looked at Rikki-tikki with the wicked snake's eyes that never change their expression, whatever the snake may be thinking of.

"Who is Nag?" he said. "*I* am Nag. The great god Brahm put his mark upon all our people when the first cobra spread his hood to keep the sun off Brahm as he slept. Look, and be afraid!"

He spread out his hood more than ever, and Rikki-tikki saw the spectacle mark on the back of it that looks exactly like the eye part of a hook-and-eye fastening. He was afraid for the minute; but it is impossible for a mongoose to stay frightened for

---

Vo·cab·u·lary

cowered (KOW urd) shrank back in fear

any length of time, and though Rikki-tikki had never met a live cobra before, his mother had fed him on dead ones, and he knew that all a grown mongoose's business in life was to fight and eat snakes. Nag knew that too, and at the bottom of his cold heart he was afraid.

"Well," said Rikki-tikki, and his tail began to fluff up again, "marks or no marks, do you think it is right for you to eat <u>fledglings</u> out of a nest?"

Nag was thinking to himself, and watching the least little movement in the grass behind Rikki-tikki. He knew that mongooses in the garden meant death sooner or later for him and his family, but he wanted to get Rikki-tikki off his guard. So he dropped his head a little and put it on one side.

"Let's us talk," he said. "You eat eggs. Why should not I eat birds?"

"Behind you! Look behind you!" sang Darzee.

Rikki-tikki knew better than to waste time in staring. He jumped up in the air as high as he could go, and just under him whizzed by the head of Nagaina, Nag's wicked wife. She had crept up behind him as he was talking, to make an end of him; and he heard her savage hiss as the stroke missed. He came down almost across the back, and if he had been an old mongoose, he would have known that then was the time to break her back with one bite; but he was afraid of the terrible lashing return stroke of the cobra. He bit, indeed, but did not bite long enough, and he jumped clear of the whisking tail, leaving Nagaina torn and angry.

"Wicked, wicked Darzee!" said Nag, lashing up as high as he could reach toward the nest in the thornbush; but Darzee had built it out of the reach of snakes, and it only swayed to and fro.

Rikki-tikki felt his eyes growing red and hot (when a mongoose's eyes grow red, he is angry), and he sat back on his tail

Vo·cab·u·lary

fledglings (FLEJ lings) young birds that haven't yet grown the feathers needed to fly

and hind legs like a little kangaroo, and looked all around him, and chattered with rage. But Nag and Nagaina had disappeared into the grass. When a snake misses its stroke, it never says anything or gives any sign of what it means to do next. Rikki-tikki did not care to follow them, for he did not feel sure that he could manage two snakes at once. So he trotted off to the gravel path near the house, and sat down to think. It was a serious matter for him. ❸

❸ Reviewing
Which animals are Rikki-tikki's friends? Which are not?

If you read the old books of natural history, you will find they say that when the mongoose fights the snake and happens to be bitten, he runs off and eats some herb that cures him. That is not true. The victory is only a matter of quickness of eye and quickness of foot—snake's blow against mongoose's jump—and as no eye can follow the motion of a snake's head when it strikes, that makes things much more wonderful than any magic herb. Rikki-tikki knew he was a young mongoose, and it made him all the more pleased to think that he had managed to escape a blow from behind. It gave him confidence in himself, and when Teddy came running down the path, Rikki-tikki was ready to be petted.

But just as Teddy was stooping, something <u>flinched</u> a little in the dust, and a tiny voice said: "Be careful. I am death!" It was Karait, the dusty brown snakeling that lies for choice on the dusty earth; and his bite is as dangerous as the cobra's. But he is so small that nobody thinks of him, and so he does the more harm to people.

Rikki-tikki's eyes grew red again, and he danced up to Karait with the peculiar rocking, swaying motion that he had inherited from his family. It looks very funny, but it is so perfectly balanced a <u>gait</u> that you can fly off from it at any angle you please; and in dealing with snakes this is an advantage. If Rikki-tikki had only

---

Vo•cab•u•lary

flinched (flinchd) started or winced involuntarily
gait (gayt) a particular manner of moving on foot

known, he was doing a much more dangerous thing than fighting Nag, for Karait is so small, and can turn so quickly, that unless Rikki bit him close to the back of the head, he would get the return stroke in his eye or lip. But Rikki did not know: his eyes were all red, and he rocked back and forth, looking for a good place to hold. Karait struck out. Rikki jumped sideways and tried to run in, but the the wicked little dusty gray head lashed within a fraction of his shoulder, and he had to jump over the body, and the head followed his heels close.

Teddy shouted to the house: "Oh, look here! Our mongoose is killing a snake"; and Rikki-tikki heard a scream from Teddy's mother. His father ran out with a stick, but by the time he came up, Karait had <u>lunged</u> out once too far, and Rikki-tikki had sprung, jumped on the snake's back, dropped his head far between his forelegs, bitten as high up the back as he could get hold, and rolled away. That bite paralyzed Karait, and Rikki-tikki was just going to eat him up from the tail, after the custom of his family at dinner, when he remembered that a full meal makes a slow mongoose, and if he wanted all his strength and quickness ready, he must keep himself thin.

He went away for a dust bath under the castor-oil bushes, while Teddy's father beat the dead Karait. "What is the use of that?" thought Rikki-tikki. "I have settled it all"; and then Teddy's mother picked him up from the dust and hugged him, crying that he had saved Teddy from death, and Teddy's father said that he was a <u>providence</u>, and Teddy looked on with big scared

Vo•cab•u•lary

lunged (lunjd) moved forward suddenly
providence (PROV ih dens) a blessing from God or nature

eyes. Rikki-tikki was rather amused at all the fuss, which, of course, he did not understand. Teddy's mother might just as well have petted Teddy for playing in the dust. Rikki was thoroughly enjoying himself.

That night, at dinner, walking to and fro among the wineglasses on the table, he could have stuffed himself three times over with nice things; but he remembered Nag and Nagaina, and though it was very pleasant to be patted and petted by Teddy's mother, and to sit on Teddy's shoulder, his eyes would get red from time to time, and he would go off into his long war cry of *"Rikk-tikk-tikki-tikki-tchk!"*

Teddy carried him off to bed and insisted on Rikki-tikki sleeping under his chin. Rikki-tikki was too well bred to bite or scratch, but as soon as Teddy was asleep he went off for his nightly walk round the house, and in the dark he ran up against Chuchundra, the muskrat, creeping round by the wall. Chuchundra is a broken-hearted little beast. He whimpers and cheeps all the night, trying to make up his mind to run into the middle of the room, but he never gets there.

"Don't kill me," said Chuchundra, almost weeping. "Rikki-tikki, don't kill me."

"Do you think a snake-killer kills muskrats?" said Rikki-tikki scornfully.

"Those who kill snakes get killed by snakes," said Chuchundra, more sorrowfully than ever. "And how am I to be sure that Nag won't mistake me for you some dark night?"

"There's not the least danger," said Rikki-tikki; "but Nag is in the garden, and I know you don't go there."

"My cousin Chua, the rat, told me—" said Chuchundra, and then he stopped.

"Told you what?"

"H'sh! Nag is everywhere, Rikki-tikki. You should have talked to Chua in the garden."

"I didn't—so you must tell me. Quick, Chuchundra, or I'll bite you!"

Chuchundra sat down and cried till the tears rolled off his whiskers. "I am a very poor man," he sobbed. "I never had spirit enough to run out into the middle of the room. H'sh! I mustn't tell you anything. Can't you *hear*, Rikki-tikki?"

Rikki-tikki listened. The house was as still as still but he thought he could just catch the faintest *scratch-scratch* in the world—a noise as faint as that of a wasp walking on a window pane—the dry scratch of a snake's scales on brickwork.

"That's Nag or Nagaina," he said to himself; "and he is crawling into the bathroom <u>sluice</u>. You're right, Chuchundra; I should have talked to Chua." **4**

He stole off to Teddy's bathroom, but there was nothing there, and then to Teddy's mother's bathroom. At the bottom of the smooth plaster wall there was a brick pulled out to make a sluice for the bath water, and as Rikki-tikki stole in by the masonry curb where the bath is put, he heard Nag and Nagaina whispering together outside in the moonlight.

"When the house is emptied of people," said Nagaina to her husband, "*he* will have to go away, and then the garden will be our own again. Go in quietly, and remember that the big man who killed Karait is the first one to bite. Then come out and tell me, and we will hunt for Rikki-tikki together."

"But are you sure there is anything to be gained by killing the people?" said Nag.

"Everything. When there were no people in the bungalow, did we have any mongoose in the garden? So long as the bungalow is empty, we are king and queen of the garden; and remember that as soon as our eggs in the melon bed hatch (as they may tomorrow), our children will need room and quiet."

"I had not thought of that," said Nag. "I will go, but there

> **4 Reviewing**
> How does Chuchundra help Rikki?

Vo·cab·u·lary

sluice (sloos) a drainpipe

is no need that we should hunt for Rikki-tikki afterward. I will kill the big man and his wife, and the child if I can, and come away quietly. Then the bungalow will be empty, and Rikki-tikki will go."

Rikki-tikki tingled all over with rage and hatred at this, and then Nag's head came through the sluice, and his five feet of cold body followed it. Angry as he was, Rikki-tikki was very frightened as he saw the size of the big cobra. Nag coiled himself up, raised his head, and looked into the bathroom in the dark, and Rikki could see his eyes glitter.

"Now, if I kill him there, Nagaina will know; and if I fight him on the open floor, the odds are in his favor. What am I to do?" said Rikki-tikki-tavi.

Nag waved to and fro, and then Rikki-tikki heard him drinking from the biggest water jar that was used to fill the bath. "That is good," said the snake. "Now, when Karait was killed, the big man had a stick. He may have that stick still, but when he comes in to bathe in the morning he will not have a stick. I shall wait here till he comes. Nagaina—do you hear me? I shall wait

here in the cool till daytime."

There was no answer from outside, so Rikki-tikki knew Nagaina had gone away. Nag coiled himself down, coil by coil, round the bulge at the bottom of the water jar, and Rikki-tikki stayed still as death. After an hour he began to move, muscle by muscle, toward the jar. Nag was asleep, and Rikki-tikki looked at his big back, wondering which would be the best place for a good hold. "If I don't break his back at the first jump," said Rikki, "he can still fight; and if he fights—O Rikki!" He looked at the thickness of the neck below the hood, but that was too much for him; and a bite near the tail would only make Nag savage.

"It must be the head," he said at last; "the head above the hood; and when I am once there, I must not let go."

Then he jumped. The head was lying a little clear of the water jar, under the curve of it; and as his teeth met, Rikki braced his back against the bulge of the red earthenware to hold down the head. This gave him just one second's <u>purchase</u>, and he made the most of it. Then he was battered to and fro as a rat is shaken by a dog—to and fro on the floor, up and down, and round in great circles; but his eyes were red, and he held on as the body <u>cartwhipped</u> over the floor, upsetting the tin dipper and the soap dish and the fleshbrush, and banged against the tin side of the bath. As he held, he closed his jaws tighter and tighter, for he made sure he would be banged to death, and, for the honor of his family, he preferred to be found with his teeth locked. He was dizzy, aching, and felt shaken to pieces when something went off like a thunderclap just behind him; a hot wind knocked him senseless, and red fire singed his fur. The big man had been wakened by the noise, and had fired both barrels of a shotgun into Nag just behind the hood.

Rikki-tikki held on with his eyes shut, for now he was quite sure he was dead; but the head did not move, and the big man

---

Vo•cab•u•lary

purchase (PUR chis) an advantage used to exert one's power
cartwhipped (CART whipt) thrown about like a whip

picked him up and said: "It's the mongoose again, Alice; the little chap has saved *our* lives now." Then Teddy's mother came in with a very white face, and saw what was left of Nag, and Rikki-tikki dragged himself to Teddy's bedroom and spent half the rest of the night shaking himself tenderly to find out whether he really was broken into forty pieces, as he <u>fancied</u>.

When morning came he was very stiff, but well pleased with his doings. "Now I have Nagaina to settle with, and she will be worse than five Nags, and there's no knowing when the eggs she spoke of will hatch. Goodness! I must go and see Darzee," he said.

Without waiting for breakfast, Rikki-tikki ran to the thornbush where Darzee was singing a song of triumph at the top of his voice. The news of Nag's death was all over the garden, for the sweeper had thrown the body on the rubbish heap.

"Oh, you stupid tuft of feathers!" said Rikki-tikki angrily. "Is this the time to sing?"

"Nag is dead—is dead—is dead!" sang Darzee. "The <u>valiant</u> Rikki-tikki caught him by the head and held fast. The big man brought the bang-stick, and Nag fell in two pieces! He will never eat my babies again."

"All that's true enough; but where's Nagaina?" said Rikki-tikki, looking carefully round him.

"Nagaina came to the bathroom sluice and called for Nag," Darzee went on; "and Nag came out on the end of a stick—the sweeper picked him up on the end of a stick and threw him upon the rubbish heap. Let us sing about the great, the red-eyed Rikki-tikki!" And Darzee filled his throat and sang.

"If I could get up to your nest, I'd roll all your babies out!" said Rikki-tikki. "You don't know when to do the right thing at the right time. You're safe enough in your nest there, but it's war for me down here. Stop singing a minute, Darzee."

Vo•cab•u•lary

fancied (FAN seed) imagined
valiant (VAL yent) brave; courageous

"For the great, the beautiful Rikki-tikki's sake I will stop," said Darzee. "What is it, O Killer of the terrible Nag?"

"Where is Nagaina, for the third time?"

"On the rubbish heap by the stables, mourning for Nag. Great is Rikki-tikki with the white teeth."

"Bother my white teeth![1] Have you ever heard where she keeps her eggs?"

"In the melon bed, on the end nearest the wall, where the sun strikes nearly all day. She hid them there weeks ago."

"And you never thought it worthwhile to tell me? The end nearest the wall, you said?"

"Rikki-tikki, you are not going to eat her eggs?"

"Not eat exactly; no. Darzee, if you have a grain of sense you will fly off to the stables and pretend that your wing is broken, and let Nagaina chase you away to this bush! I must get to the melon bed, and if I went there now she'd see me."

Darzee was a featherbrained little fellow who could never hold more than one idea at a time in his head; and just because he knew that Nagaina's children were born in eggs like his own, he didn't think at first that it was fair to kill them. But his wife was a sensible bird, and she knew that cobras' eggs meant young cobras later on; so she flew off from the nest, and left Darzee to keep the babies warm, and continue his song about the death of Nag. Darzee was very like a man in some ways.

She fluttered in front of Nagaina by the rubbish heap and cried out, "Oh, my wing is broken! The boy in the house threw a stone at me and broke it." Then she fluttered more desperately than ever.

Nagaina lifted up her head and hissed, "You warned Rikki-tikki when I would have killed him. Indeed and truly, you've chosen a bad place to be lame in." And she moved toward Darzee's wife, slipping along over the dust.

. . . .

[1]"Bother my white teeth" is a British way of saying, "Don't concern yourself with my teeth."

"The boy broke it with a stone!" shrieked Darzee's wife.

"Well! It may be some consolation to you when you're dead to know that I shall settle accounts with the boy. My husband lies on the rubbish heap this morning, but before night the boy in the house will lie very still. What is the use of running away? I am sure to catch you. Little fool, look at me!"

Darzee's wife knew better than to do *that*, for a bird who looks at a snake's eyes gets so frightened that she cannot move. Darzee's wife fluttered on, piping sorrowfully, and never leaving the ground, and Nagaina quickened her pace.

Rikk-tikki heard them going up the path from the stables, and

he raced for the end of the melon patch near the wall. There, in the warm litter about the melons, very cunningly hidden, he found twenty-five eggs, about the size of a bantam's eggs but with whitish skin instead of shell.

"I was not a day too soon," he said; for he could see the baby cobras curled up inside the skin, and he knew that the minute they were hatched they could each kill a man or a mongoose. He bit off the tops of the eggs as fast as he could, taking care to crush the young cobras, and turned over the litter from time to time to see whether he had missed any. **5** At last there were only three eggs left, and Rikki-tikki began to chuckle to himself, when he heard Darzee's wife screaming:

5 Reviewing
How does a mongoose rid a garden of all cobras?

"Rikki-tikki, I led Nagaina toward the house, and she has gone into the veranda, and—oh, come quickly she means killing!"

Rikki-tikki smashed two eggs, and tumbled backward down the melon bed with the third egg in his mouth, and scuttled to the veranda as hard as he could put foot to the ground. Teddy and his mother and father were there at early breakfast; but Rikki-tikki saw that they were not eating anything. They sat stone-still, and their faces were white. Nagaina was coiled up on the matting by Teddy's chair, within easy striking distance of Teddy's bare leg, and she was swaying to and fro singing a song of triumph.

"Son of the big man that killed Nag," she hissed, "stay still. I am not ready yet. Wait a little. Keep very still, all you three. If you move I strike, and if you do not move I strike. Oh, foolish people, who killed my Nag!"

Teddy's eyes were fixed on his father, and all his father could do was to whisper, "Sit still, Teddy. You mustn't move. Teddy, keep still."

Then Rikki-tikki came up and cried: "Turn round, Nagaina; turn and fight!"

"All in good time," said she, without moving her eyes. "I will settle my account with *you* presently. Look at your friends, Rikki-tikki. They are still and white; they are afraid. They dare not move, and if you come a step nearer I strike."

"Look at your eggs," said Rikki-tikki, "in the melon bed near the wall. Go and look, Nagaina."

The big snake turned half round and saw the egg on the veranda. "Ah-h! Give it to me," she said.

Rikki-tikki put his paws one on each side of the egg, and his eyes were blood-red. "What price for a snake's egg? For a young cobra? For a young king cobra? For the last—the very last of the <u>brood</u>? The ants are eating all the others down by the melon bed." **6**

6 Reviewing
How does Rikki get Nagaina's attention?

Nagaina spun clear round, forgetting everything for the sake of the one egg; and Rikki-tikki saw Teddy's father shoot out a big hand, catch Teddy by the shoulder, and drag him across the little table with the teacups, safe and out of reach of Nagaina.

"Tricked! Tricked! Tricked! *Rikki-tck-tck!*" chuckled Rikki-tikki. "The boy is safe, and it was I—I—I that caught Nag by the hood last night in the bathroom." Then he began to jump up and down, all four feet together, his head close to the floor. "He threw me to and fro, but he could not shake me off. He was dead before the big man blew him in two. I did it. *Rikk-tikki-tck-tck!* Come then, Nagaina. Come and fight with me. You shall not be a widow long."

Nagaina saw that she had lost her chance of killing Teddy, and the egg lay between Rikki-tikki's paws. "Give me the egg, Rikki-tikki. Give me the last of my eggs, and I will go away and never come back," she said, lowering her hood.

"Yes, you will go away, and you will never come back; for you will go to the rubbish heap with Nag. Fight, widow! The big man

---

Vo·cab·u·lary

brood (brood) all of the young of an animal that are born or cared for at the same time

has gone for his gun! Fight!"

Rikki-tikki was bounding all round Nagaina, keeping just out of reach of her stroke, his little eyes like hot coals. Nagaina gathered herself together and flung out at him. Rikki-tikki jumped up and backward. Again and again and again she struck, and each time her head came with a whack on the matting of the veranda, and she gathered herself together like a watch-spring. Then Rikki-tikki danced in a circle to get behind her, and Nagaina spun round to keep her head to his head, so that the rustle of her tail on the matting sounded like dry leaves blown along by the wind.

He had forgotten the egg. It still lay on the veranda, and Nagaina came nearer and nearer to it, till at last, while Rikki-tikki was drawing breath, she caught it in her mouth, turned to the veranda steps, and flew like an arrow down the path, with Rikki-tikki behind her. When the cobra runs for her life, she goes like a whiplash flicked across a horse's neck.

Rikki-tikki knew that he must catch her, or all the trouble would begin again. She headed straight for the long grass by the thornbush, and as he was running Rikki-tikki heard Darzee

singing his foolish little song of triumph. But Darzee's wife was wiser. She flew off her nest as Nagaina came along, and flapped her wings about Nagaina's head. If Darzee had helped they might have turned her; but Nagaina only lowered her hood and went on. Still, the instant's delay brought Rikki-tikki up to her, and as she plunged into the rat hole where she and Nag used to live, his little white teeth were clenched on her tail, and he went down with her—and very few mongooses, however wise and old they may be, care to follow a cobra into its hole. It was dark in the hole; and Rikki-tikki never knew when it might open out and give Nagaina room to turn and strike at him. He held on savagely and stuck out his feet to act as brakes on the dark slope of the hot, moist earth.

Then the grass by the mouth of the hole stopped waving, and Darzee said: "It is all over with Rikki-tikki! We must sing his death song. Valiant Rikki-tikki is dead. For Nagaina will surely kill him underground."

So he sang a very mournful song that he made up all on the spur of the minute, and just as he got to the most touching part the grass quivered again, and Rikki-tikki, covered with dirt, dragged himself out of the hole leg by leg, licking his whiskers. Darzee stopped with a little shout. Rikki-tikki shook some of the dust out of his fur and sneezed. "It is all over," he said. "The widow will never come out again." And the red ants that live between the grass stems heard him, and began to troop down one after another to see if he had spoken the truth.

Rikki-tikki curled himself up in the grass and slept where he was—slept and slept till it was late in the afternoon, for he had done a hard day's work.

"Now," he said, when he awoke, "I will go back to the house. Tell the coppersmith, Darzee, and he will tell the garden that Nagaina is dead."

The coppersmith is a bird who makes a noise exactly like the beating of a little hammer on a copper pot; and the reason he is always making it is because he is the town crier to every Indian garden, and tells all the news to everybody who cares to listen. As Rikki-tikki went up the path, he heard his "attention" notes like a tiny dinner gong; and then the steady "*Ding-dong-tock! Nag is dead—dong! Nagaina is dead! Ding-dong-tock!*" That set all the birds in the garden singing, and the frogs croaking, for Nag and Nagaina used to eat frogs as well as little birds.

When Rikki got to the house, Teddy and Teddy's mother (she still looked very white, for she had been fainting) and Teddy's father came out and almost cried over him; and that night he ate all that was given him till he could eat no more, and went to bed on Teddy's shoulder, where Teddy's mother saw him when she came to look late at night.

"He saved our lives and Teddy's life," she said to her husband. "Just think, he saved all our lives!"

Rikki-tikki woke up with a jump, for all mongooses are light sleepers.

"Oh, it's you," said he. "What are you bothering for? All the cobras are dead; and if they weren't, I'm here."

Rikki-tikki had a right to be proud of himself; but he did not grow too proud, and he kept that garden as a mongoose should keep it, with tooth and jump and spring and bite, till never a cobra dared show its head inside the walls. **7** ○

> **7 Reviewing**
> How does Rikki spread the word about his victory over the cobras?

Answering the
BIG Question

As you do the following activities, consider the Big Question:
Why do we read?

WRITE TO LEARN What did you already know about a mongoose before you read this story? What new information did you learn? Write a brief entry in your Learner's Notebook.

LITERATURE GROUPS Meet with two or three others who have also read "Rikki-tikki-tavi." Discuss your responses to the main characters. What kept each of you reading?

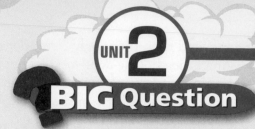

How can we become who we want to be?

In this unit, you will read the stories of real people and fictional characters. These stories may inspire you to give your own answer to the question: *How can we become who we want to be?*

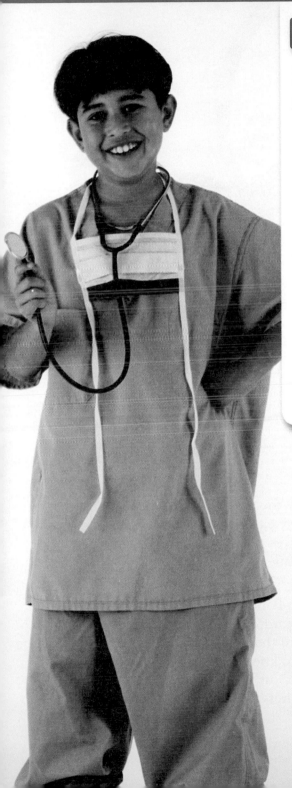

Key Reading Skills

As you read the selections in this unit, apply these reading skills.

- **Activating Prior Knowledge** Think about any information you already know that might help you understand the selection.

- **Connecting** Ask yourself: How are the events in the selection similar to or different from events in my life?

- **Inferring** Use your thought processes and experiences to understand the character's and the author's message.

- **Understanding Sequence** Find the logical order of ideas or events in a selection.

THE NO-GUITAR BLUES

by Gary Soto

What happens when an honest person wants something so badly he'll lie to get it?

The moment Fausto saw the group Los Lobos on "American Bandstand," he knew exactly what he wanted to do with his life—play guitar. His eyes grew large with excitement as Los Lobos ground out a song while teenagers bounced off each other on the crowded dance floor.

He had watched "American Bandstand" for years and had heard Ray Camacho and the Teardrops at Romain Playground, but it had never occurred to him that he too might become a musician. That afternoon Fausto knew his mission in life: to play guitar in his own band; to sweat out his songs and prance around the stage; to make money and dress weird.

Fausto turned off the television set and walked outside, wondering how he could get enough money to buy a guitar. He couldn't ask his parents because they would just say, "Money doesn't grow on trees" or "What do you think we are, bankers?" And besides, they hated rock music. They were into the *conjunto* music of Lydia Mendoza, Flaco Jimenez, and Little Joe and La Familia. And, as Fausto recalled, the last <u>album</u> they bought was *The Chipmunks Sing Christmas Favorites*. ❶

But what the heck, he'd give it a try. He returned inside and watched his mother make tortillas. He leaned against the kitchen counter, trying to work up the nerve to ask her for a guitar. Finally, he couldn't hold back any longer.

❶ **Connecting**
When has an adult responded to a request you made in words like those Fausto's parents used?

"Mom," he said, "I want a guitar for Christmas."

She looked up from rolling tortillas. "Honey, a guitar costs a lot of money."

"How 'bout for my birthday next year," he tried again.

"I can't promise," she said, turning back to her tortillas, "but we'll see."

Fausto walked back outside with a buttered tortilla. He knew his mother was right. His father was a warehouseman at Berven Rugs, where he made good money but not enough to buy everything his children wanted. Fausto decided to mow lawns to earn money, and was pushing the mower down the street before he realized it was winter and no one would hire him. He returned the mower and picked up a rake. He hopped onto his sister's bike (his had two flat tires) and rode north to the nicer section of Fresno in search of work. He went door-to-door, but after three hours he managed to get only one job, and not to rake leaves. He was asked to hurry down to the store to buy a loaf of bread, for which he received a grimy, dirt-caked quarter.

Vo·cab·u·lary

album (AL bum) music recording on a 12-inch vinyl disc

He also got an orange, which he ate sitting at the curb. While he was eating, a dog walked up and sniffed his leg. Fausto pushed him away and threw an orange peel skyward. The dog caught it and ate it in one gulp. The dog looked at Fausto and wagged his tail for more. Fausto tossed him a slice of orange, and the dog snapped it up and licked his lips.

"How come you like oranges, dog?"

The dog blinked a pair of sad eyes and whined.

"What's the matter? Cat got your tongue?" Fausto laughed at his joke and offered the dog another slice.

At that moment a dim light came on inside Fausto's head. He saw that it was sort of a fancy dog, a terrier or something, with dog tags and a shiny collar. And it looked well fed and healthy. In his neighborhood, the dogs were never licensed, and if they got sick they were placed near the water heater until they got well.

This dog looked like he belonged to rich people. Fausto cleaned his juice-sticky hands on his pants and got to his feet. The light in his head grew brighter. It just might work. He called the dog, patted its muscular back, and bent down to check the license.

"Great," he said. "There's an address."

The dog's name was Roger, which struck Fausto as weird because he'd never heard of a dog with a human name. Dogs should have names like Bomber, Freckles, Queenie, Killer, and Zero.

Fausto planned to take the dog home and collect a reward. He would say he had found Roger near the freeway. That would scare the daylights out of the owners, who would be so happy that they would probably give him a reward. He felt bad about lying, but the dog *was* loose. And it might even really be lost, because the address was six blocks away.

Fausto stashed the rake and his sister's bike behind a bush, and, tossing an orange peel every time Roger became distracted, walked the dog to his house. He hesitated on the porch until Roger began to scratch the door with a muddy paw. Fausto had come this far, so he figured he might as well go through with it. He knocked softly. When no one answered, he rang the doorbell. A man in a silky bathrobe and slippers opened the door and seemed confused by the sight of his dog and the boy.

"Sir," Fausto said, gripping Roger by the collar. "I found your dog by the freeway. His dog license says he lives here." Fausto looked down at the dog, then up to the man. "He does, doesn't he?"

The man stared at Fausto a long time before saying in a pleasant voice, "That's right." He pulled his robe tighter around him because of the cold and asked Fausto to come in. "So he was by the freeway?"

"Uh-huh."

"You bad, snoopy dog," said the man, wagging his finger. "You probably knocked over some trash cans, too, didn't you?"

Fausto didn't say anything. He looked around, amazed by this house with its shiny furniture and a television as large as the front window at home. Warm bread smells filled the air and music full of soft tinkling floated in from another room.

"Helen," the man called to the kitchen. "We have a visitor." His wife came into the living room wiping her hands on a dish towel and smiling. "And who have we here?" she asked in one of the softest voices Fausto had ever heard.

"This young man said he found Roger near the freeway." Fausto repeated his story to her while staring at a <u>perpetual</u> clock with a bell-shaped glass, the kind his aunt got when she celebrated her twenty-fifth anniversary. The lady frowned and said, wagging a finger at Roger, "Oh, you're a bad boy."

"It was very nice of you to bring Roger home," the man said. "Where do you live?"

"By that vacant lot on Olive," he said. "You know, by Brownie's Flower Place."

The wife looked at her husband, then Fausto. Her eyes twinkled triangles of light as she said, "Well, young man, you're probably hungry. How about a turnover?"

Vo•cab•u•lary

perpetual (pur PECH oo ul) continuing forever

"What do I have to turn over?" Fausto asked, thinking she was talking about yard work or something like turning trays of dried raisins.

"No, no, dear, it's a pastry." She took him by the elbow and guided him to a kitchen that sparkled with copper pans and bright yellow wallpaper. She guided him to the kitchen table and gave him a tall glass of milk and something that looked like an *empanada*. Steamy waves of heat escaped when he tore it in two. He ate with both eyes on the man and woman who stood arm-in-arm smiling at him. They were strange, he thought. But nice.

"That was good," he said after he finished the turnover. "Did you make it, ma'am?"

"Yes, I did. Would you like another?"

"No, thank you. I have to go home now."

As Fausto walked to the door, the man opened his wallet and took out a bill. "This is for you," he said. "Roger is special to us, almost like a son."

Fausto looked at the bill and knew he was in trouble. Not with these nice folks or with his parents but with himself. How could he have been so <u>deceitful</u>? The dog wasn't lost. It was just having a fun Saturday walking around.

"I can't take that."

"You have to. You deserve it, believe me," the man said.

"No, I don't." **2**

"Now don't be silly," said the lady. She took the bill from her husband and stuffed it into Fausto's shirt pocket. "You're a lovely child. Your parents are lucky to have you. Be good. And come see us again, please."

> **2 Inferring**
> Why did Fausto try to refuse the reward that Roger's family offered him?

Vo·cab·u·lary

deceitful (dee SEET ful) not honest

Fausto went out, and the lady closed the door. Fausto clutched the bill through his shirt pocket. He felt like ringing the doorbell and begging them to please take the money back, but he knew they would refuse. He hurried away, and at the end of the block, pulled the bill from his shirt pocket: it was a crisp twenty-dollar bill.

"Oh, man, I shouldn't have lied," he said under his breath as he started up the street like a zombie. He wanted to run to church for Saturday confession, but it was past four-thirty, when confession stopped.

He returned to the bush where he had hidden the rake and his sister's bike and rode home slowly, not daring to touch the money in his pocket. At home, in the privacy of his room, he examined the twenty-dollar bill. He had never had so much money. It was probably enough to buy a secondhand guitar. But he felt bad, like the time he stole a dollar from the secret fold inside his older brother's wallet.

Fausto went outside and sat on the fence. "Yeah," he said. "I can probably get a guitar for twenty. Maybe at a yard sale—things are cheaper."

His mother called him to dinner.

The next day he dressed for church without anyone telling him. He was going to go to eight o'clock mass.

"I'm going to church, Mom," he said. His mother was in the kitchen cooking _papas_ and _chorizo con huevos_. A pile of tortillas lay warm under a dish towel.

"Oh, I'm so proud of you, Son." She beamed, turning over the crackling _papas_.

His older brother, Lawrence, who was at the table reading the funnies, _mimicked_, "Oh, I'm so proud of you, my son," under his breath.

At Saint Theresa's he sat near the front. When Father Jerry began by saying that we are all sinners, Fausto thought he looked right at him. Could he know? Fausto fidgeted with guilt. No, he thought. I only did it yesterday.

Fausto knelt, prayed, and sang. But he couldn't forget the man and the lady, whose names he didn't even know, and the _empanada_ they had given him. It had a strange name but tasted really good. He wondered how they got rich. And how that dome clock worked. He had asked his mother once how his aunt's clock worked. She said it just worked, the way the refrigerator works. It just did.

Fausto caught his mind wandering and tried to concentrate on his sins. He said a Hail Mary and sang, and when the wicker basket came his way, he stuck a hand reluctantly in his pocket and pulled out the twenty-dollar bill. He ironed it between his palms,

Vo•cab•u•lary

papas (PAH pahs) Spanish for potatoes
chorizo con huevos (choh REE soh kohn WAY vohs) Spanish for sausage with eggs
mimicked (MIM ikt) imitated closely

and dropped it into the basket. The grown-ups stared. Here was a kid dropping twenty dollars in the basket while they gave just three or four dollars. **3**

3 Connecting
In what ways have you tried to relieve a guilty conscience?

There would be a second collection for Saint Vincent de Paul, the lector announced. The wicker baskets again floated in the pews, and this time the adults around him, given a second chance to show their charity, dug deep into their wallets and purses and dropped in fives and tens. This time Fausto tossed in the grimy quarter.

Fausto felt better after church. He went home and played football in the front yard with his brother and some neighbor kids. He felt cleared of wrongdoing and was so happy that he played one of his best games of football ever. On one play, he tore his good pants, which he knew he shouldn't have been wearing. For a second, while he examined the hole, he wished he hadn't given the twenty dollars away.

Man, I coulda bought me some Levi's, he thought. He pictured his twenty dollars being spent to buy church candles. He pictured a priest buying an armful of flowers with his money.

Fausto had to forget about getting a guitar. He spent the next day playing soccer in his good pants, which were now his old pants. But that night during dinner, his mother said she remembered seeing an old bass <u>guitarron</u> the last time she cleaned out her father's garage.

"It's a little dusty," his mom said, serving his favorite enchiladas, "but I think it works. Grandpa says it works."

Fausto's ears perked up. That was the same kind the guy in Los Lobos played. Instead of asking for the guitar, he waited for his mother to offer it to him. And she did, while gathering the dishes from the table.

"No, Mom, I'll do it," he said, hugging her. "I'll do the dishes forever if you want."

Vo•cab•u•lary

guitarron (gee tah ROHN) a type of guitar

It was the happiest day of his life. No, it was the second-happiest day of his life. The happiest was when his grandfather Lupe placed the guitarron, which was nearly as huge as a washtub, in his arms. Fausto ran a thumb down the strings, which vibrated in his throat and chest. It sounded beautiful, deep and eerie. A pumpkin smile widened on his face.

"OK, *hijo*, now you put your fingers like this," said his grandfather, smelling of tobacco and aftershave. He took Fausto's fingers and placed them on the strings. Fausto strummed a chord on the guitarron, and the bass resounded in their chests.

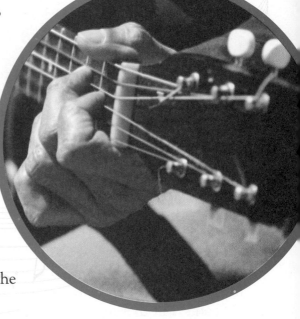

The guitarron was more complicated than Fausto imagined. But he was confident that after a few more lessons he could start a band that would someday play on "American Bandstand" for the dancing crowds. ○

Answering the BIG Question

As you do the following activities, consider the Big Question:
How can we become who we want to be?

WRITE TO LEARN Write a brief entry in your Learner's Notebook about how Fausto handled the guilt he felt after lying. How else could he have solved his problem?

PARTNER TALK Get together with another student who has read this selection. Discuss some situations in which a person's honesty might be tested.

Merrick Johnston, Mountain Climber

by Merrick Johnston

What is it like to climb the highest mountain in North America when you're only eleven years old?

Because my entire state (Alaska) is one big playground, anytime I want an adventure, all I have to do is look in my own backyard. I've taken all of my friends on hikes, giving many of them their first true taste of Alaska. I think that many people who live here haven't learned to appreciate what this place has to offer; they seem to spend most of their time inside their houses or driving in their cars. If you get to know Alaska's <u>terrain</u>, life here can be extraordinary.

Hiking and spending time in the mountains are my favorite things to do. My mom runs her own company, Great Alaskan Gourmet Adventures, organizing adventures for people who want

Vo•cab•u•lary
terrain (tur RAYN) the type of land

to explore the outdoors. I work with her as a guide. Together, we teach clients hiking and technical skills for rock and ice climbing, and we take them on all kinds of trips to places like Prospect Heights, Wolverine Peak, and Little Switzerland. I've always loved hanging out with the mountaineers I've met through my mom's business. When I hear about their experiences, I think about the things I may be able to accomplish someday. Best of all, working as a guide has exposed me to the joy of mountain climbing at an early age.

When I was nine, I heard one of the more experienced climbers describe what it was like to scale Mount McKinley—the unpredictable climate; the challenging, icy terrain; the awesome feeling of reaching the summit. My interest was sparked right away.

Denali (Mt. McKinley's Indian name) is the highest peak in North America. At 20,320 feet, its arctic conditions make climbing Mt. McKinley a major test of personal strength, technical skill, and teamwork. I dreamed of climbing that icy peak—all I had to do was convince my mom I could!

Two years later, I finally won her over. My mom realized that I was serious about attempting "The High One," as Mt. McKinley is called. I was determined to become the youngest person to accomplish this feat (beating the boy who set the record before me).

I grew up with two older brothers, and most of my friends were boys. You might say I was just "one of the guys." I did everything they did, and more. By the time I was eight, I realized many girls were interested in different activities than boys. I also learned that the boys I hung out with thought they were naturally better athletes than the girls they knew. Well, this fired up my competitive spirit. I wanted to prove girls can do anything, and this helped fuel my desire to climb Mt. McKinley.

Although my mom had given in to my <u>pleas</u> to make the

Vo•cab•u•lary

pleas (pleez) appeals or requests

climb, she said I couldn't go on the expedition alone. We decided to attempt the ascent together, along with an experienced group of climbers. I knew I needed to be strong and fit to take on such a huge challenge.

I was already physically active, spending as much time as I could enjoying outdoor activities like skiing, snowboarding, canoeing, hiking, and rafting. I also played soccer, ran track, and did gymnastics. But it's not just fitness that counts when climbing: You must also have excellent mountaineering skills. On a mountain like Denali, I'd be facing life-threatening situations. If I didn't know what I was doing, I'd pose a threat to myself and to everyone else participating in the climb. ❶

❶ Connecting In what situations might other people depend on your strength and skill?

To help prepare for the expedition, my mom and I practiced our glacier-travel techniques, winter camping skills, and climbing with *crampons* (metal spikes clamped onto our boots). We also climbed Alaska's Mount Goode—a 10,900 foot peak in the Chugach Mountains—to test my high-altitude and cold-weather endurance. My mom trained with me daily on the Chugach Range, where I climbed with a 50-pound pack on my back. This helped build my strength and <u>stamina</u>, both of which are important for high-altitude climbing in cold conditions. Because the altitude can zap your strength, it's essential to develop deep reserves of energy to draw from.

We also became familiar with "crevasse rescue" (a crevasse is basically a deep crevice, often found in a glacier). Because glaciers are like large rivers that flow, ebb, and shift, deep crevasses form as the glaciers travel downward. The crevasses can be hundreds of feet deep, and if you fall in and are knocked unconscious, your climbing team must have the skills to haul you up safely with ropes. Scaling mountains has always been a fun way for me to

Vo•cab•u•lary

stamina (STA min uh) staying power; endurance

spend time. I enjoy the struggles and obstacles I face on the way up, and I like making decisions about the routes.

Mountain climbing gives me a whole different perspective on the world. When I'm on a mountain, I don't worry about any of the things that I worry about at home. I block out the rest of the world and just focus on the next step. I concentrate on my basic needs—having enough food and water, how the weather will affect the climb, planning the next step, obstacles that may lie ahead. It's all about survival, self-reliance, and instinct.

My hiking and climbing experiences have taught me the importance of enjoying the moment. If your only concern is getting to the end of the hike or the top of the mountain, you miss out on all of the wonderful things that happen along the way. Whenever I reach the peak of a mountain, I make a point of enjoying the view and the beauty of my natural surroundings. This means a lot more than just congratulating myself on getting to the top.

After I started preparing for the climb of my dreams, I discovered that my source of motivation had totally changed. Suddenly breaking a record no longer mattered to me. My new goal was simply to enjoy the climb. I also decided the climb shouldn't just be about me, so I collected pledges to raise money

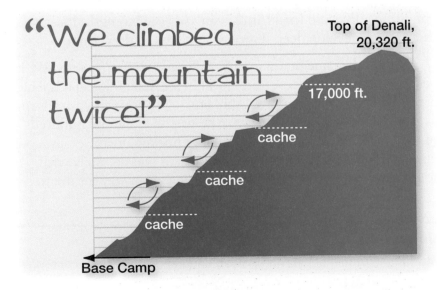

"We climbed the mountain twice!"

Top of Denali, 20,320 ft.

17,000 ft.

cache

cache

cache

Base Camp

for a wellness and child-abuse-prevention center in Anchorage. The higher I climbed, the more money I'd raise for a good cause.

On June 1, 1995, we began our ascent to Denali's summit. Our group consisted of eight people, and we divided into two teams of four.

We carried enough food and fuel to weather any storms. Because hauling a lot of extra gear on our backs was difficult, we regularly loaded up sleds that held our extra food and fuel, then towed the sleds up about 1,000 feet, so we could bury the supplies. Then we returned to our starting point to spend the night.

The next day, if the weather was good, we'd climb to the place where our supplies were buried and begin the entire process again. (So, in a sense, we climbed the mountain twice!) This process took longer, but it gave our bodies a chance to become <u>acclimated</u> to the higher altitude, which meant a better night's sleep. Plus, if we were to get stuck on the mountain due to bad weather, we'd have enough supplies to last for a while.

I discovered that the worst thing to do while hiking up the mountain was to count my footsteps; once I started, it seemed I couldn't stop. Quite frequently on our ascent, I found myself counting my footsteps for hours. I'd try to occupy my mind by singing songs with my friend J.T., who hiked close to me. This helped me stop the endless counting, and I enjoyed the journey more. ❷

❷ Inferring
What effect did counting steps have on the climbers?

As we made our way up the mountain, the weather was so bad that we had to stop for days at a time. Although it was June, the temperature hovered around 10 to 15 degrees during the day, and when the wind was blowing, the temperature dropped well below zero. Of the twenty-six days it took to complete the climb, we spent a total of thirteen unable to move.

We dug snow caves for shelter against dangerous blizzards.

Vo•cab•u•lary

acclimated (AK lih may tud) adjusted

Inside the caves, we waited for the storms to end. At 17,200 feet, we had to stay in one spot for seven days in a row. We passed the time playing cards, reading, and singing songs.

We encountered some scary *whiteouts* on the trip. Whiteouts are usually caused by blizzards or extreme snowfall (sometimes by fog). When you're caught in a whiteout, you can't tell where the sky stops and the snow on the mountainside begins.

If I'm familiar with the area in which I'm climbing, whiteouts don't bother me (it's actually kind of fun to make a game out of looking for my friends). But one of the whiteouts we encountered on Denali was so intense that I could barely see my own feet.

When the whiteout hit, we were walking on a high ridge. The snow was coming down hard, and the temperature had plummeted to about 20 degrees below zero. I told myself to keep moving. I wasn't afraid, perhaps because I focused on walking instead of thinking about the danger I was in. Looking back, I remember the whiteout as a fun and <u>exhilarating</u> experience, although most of the team was scared.

The climb proved to be eventful in other ways, too. One day, we were on a ridge 3,000 feet above a crevasse. Everyone was in a bad mood because we were tired and cold (so cold that our eyelashes had frozen). Suddenly I lost my footing and slipped, falling toward the crevasse. As I slid, I reached out and by sheer luck, grabbed my mom's ax, which was stuck in the ice. I was extremely fortunate and fell only a short distance. Who knows how far I could have dropped!

As we approached 11,000 feet on our ascent, I had an even worse scare. Some of my gear was hanging on cords around my neck, including my lip balm, a Swiss army knife, and my sunscreen. The cords somehow got tangled up in the rope that was attached to my chest harness. Before I knew what was happening, the cords were strangling me. I started choking, and I

Vo•cab•u•lary

exhilarating (ek ZIL uh ray ting) refreshing; exciting

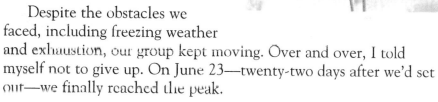

tried to yell for help. The wind howled so loudly that no one could hear my cries.

I got scared and began hyperventilating, which frightened me more. Fortunately, the other team caught up to ours, saw what was happening, and helped me get untangled. It took a few minutes for me to calm down and breathe normally again, but I was ready to continue the climb.

Despite the obstacles we faced, including freezing weather and exhaustion, our group kept moving. Over and over, I told myself not to give up. On June 23—twenty-two days after we'd set out—we finally reached the peak.

What an amazing sight! We stood speechless, staring at the incredible view and the sunset that colored the clouds pink. I'll never forget how pure everything looked from Denali's summit. I huddled next to my mom, feeling awed and, most of all, proud. I had become the youngest person to climb Mt. McKinley, setting a new record.

Later, as we made our way down, I cried. Denali was so extraordinary, and I didn't want to leave it behind. For me, mountains are like a <u>sanctuary</u>, a place where I get to know myself. It's hard to explain how I feel in the mountains. All I know is I feel wonderful.

How I got started:

A famous climber who visited my mom described the experience of climbing Mt. McKinley: This gave me the fever

---

Vo•cab•u•lary

sanctuary (SANG chu ary) a sacred or special place

to climb it myself. Plus, I've always loved outdoor challenges.

Accomplishments:

I raised $3,800 for the Anchorage Center for Families, as a result of my climb. I'm a snowboarder, too—I won second overall in combined slalom and giant slalom in the 1997 National Snowboard Race (a slalom race is a course that tests precision, speed, and flexibility; the giant slalom is designed to test speed, strength, and tenacity). I recently qualified as a member of the USASA Junior National Snowboard Team.

How I stay motivated:

What motivates me is a desire to have fun, and I want to share this enthusiasm with other people. I give talks at schools to inspire other kids to take advantage of the natural world that surrounds them and not take for granted what's right outside their back door.

My future:

I love to stay busy while having fun. My goals are to go to Dartmouth College, go hang gliding off Mount Logan (in Canada's Yukon Territory), be the youngest person to climb Vinson Massif in Antarctica, go parasailing with my snowboard, and enjoy my life. ○

Answering the BIG Question

As you do the following activities, consider the Big Question:
How can we become who we want to be?

WRITE TO LEARN Merrick decided on her goal when she heard other climbers talking about Mount McKinley. What are some other ways people discover their dream? How can you take steps to pursue a goal? Write a response in your Learner's Notebook.

LITERATURE GROUPS Join two or three other students who have read this selection. Discuss the character traits needed to become a successful mountain climber. Use examples from the selection to back up your answer.

Krumping

IF YOU LOOK LIKE BOZO HAVING SPASMS, YOU'RE DOING IT RIGHT

by Shaheem Reid,
with additional reporting by Mark Bella

Find out why it's cool to be a dancing clown.

We've been deprived all these years. We've never seen Krusty the Clown popping his booty, Ronald McDonald never C-walked, and Bozo . . . forget about it. He could probably barely do a jig, let alone shake his whole body like an enraged zombie from *28 Days Later*. **1**

Well, the dark ages are over. There's a group of California clowns doing the thang.

> **1 Activating Prior Knowledge**
> What do you know about krumping?

89

Krumping

We've gotten a <u>potent</u> <u>dosage</u> of clown dancing—or krumping, as it's called—in videos such as Missy Elliott's "I'm Really Hot" and the Black Eyed Peas, "Hey Mama." Now the ringleader of the crunk circus act says the mainstream had better look out, because he's bringing more than balloons and giant shoes. The krumping era just may be upon us.

"The clowning and the krumping dance movement, it is a very positive thing because it really does keep kids off the streets," krumping originator Thomas Johnson, a.k.a. Tommy the Clown, explained in Los Angeles recently. "Kids really don't have too much to do around here. This is something exciting for them. To Missy and everybody that has grabbed this whole clowning, krumping, hip-hop style of clown dancing, I want to say thank you for putting it on the national scale. You're doing it."

"I heard about it through ['I'm Really Hot' director] Bryan Barber," Missy Elliott said. "I knew about—we call it clown dancing—but the krumping already. We was already familiar with the dance, but he told me about the painting [of the faces], 'cause he has cousins that do it. I see people doing the dance, but I'd never seen them painted with it. I thought it would be hot for my video."

Painting is almost as important to krumping as the dance moves themselves.

"I like to do either a fade or a scenery," said one of Tommy's dancers, Rocko, as he made himself up in the mirror. "This would be like a scenery or a picture of a whale jumping outta the water into the sun. A fade would be . . . different colors just fading into each other. But there's all types of face paints you could do."

"It just comes to your head and you try to put it together," Tommy said. "Basically we try to mix it up. Different faces, different styles. It's something you gotta do."

Vo•cab•u•lary

potent (POH tent) strong
dosage (DOH sij) an exposure to some experience in a measured amount

Larry Berry, left and Marquisa Gardner—stars of David LaChappelle's latest documentary film—demonstrate a Krump dance move.

Tommy started clown dancing in Compton in 1992 as a way to entertain at birthday parties he performed at. Tommy eventually started getting his pied piper on, enlisting people from the neighborhood to come perform with him at the functions, <u>dubbing</u> themselves the Hip-Hop Clowns. The dance form eventually evolved into what he calls krumping.

"Krumping is when you're dancing and your body is doing a lot of different moves," Tommy explained. "It's really like you're fighting on the dance floor. It's more of an intensity. It can be fast-paced, it can be a lot of moves that are really sharp."

Word of mouth spread over the years, giving Tommy a chance to build his organization and set up local competitions with the kids, the most <u>prevalent</u> being Tommy the Clown's Battle Zone, where

Vo·cab·u·lary

dubbing (DUB bing) naming
prevalent (PREV uh lent) widely known

the kids square off for belts like they do in wrestling. The battling didn't just stay contained to Tommy-sanctioned events as different painted-face crews started popping up around Cali and facing off.

Many of the inner-city kids who have participated say the dancing has kept them away from some potential pitfalls.

"Me, personally, I like to be around [little] kids, I like to make them happy," said Rocko, 19, who's been clown dancing for over three years. "Besides that, it keeps me busy. It gives me something to do. It's positive. That's why I do it, pretty much."

Milk, 17, who appears in Missy's "I'm Really Hot" video and has been krumping for a year and half, agrees. "It just keeps us from doing everything negative—staying outta trouble, keeping yourself busy."

Director/photographer David LaChappelle (*NSYNC, *No Doubt*) directed and produced a documentary on the dance craze last year called *Clowns in the Hood*, which was renamed *Krumped* and premiered at this year's Sundance Film Festival.

"Man, it feels really good to be a part of this hip-hop culture movement," Tommy, the self-appointed "King of Clowns," beamed. "You would never imagine black hip-hop clowns really doing nothing until I brought it to this world. God allowed me to bring it to this world to where it has become a major movement." ○

Answering the BIG Question

As you do the following activities, consider the Big Question:
How can we become who we want to be?

WRITE TO LEARN Imagine you could put two totally unrelated things together to create a movement of your own. What would you choose? Write a brief entry in your Learner's Notebook about this new combination.

LITERATURE GROUPS Join two or three other students who have read this selection on krumping. Discuss the positive aspects of this new fad and the effect it is having on teens.

Chicago Kids Sink Their Teeth into

DINO CAMP

by Sarah Ives

Imagine traveling across the country to dig up dinosaur remains.

What are you doing this summer? For 14 kids from Chicago, the answer is digging for dinosaurs.

The Junior Paleontologist program run by Project Exploration is much more than your typical summer camp. The program gives kids a taste of what it's like to be a paleontologist. A paleontologist (pail-ee-on-TAWL-o-gist) is a scientist who studies fossils for clues about life in the distant past.

"It's a program about finding your passion," Conor Barnes, a youth-programs manager, said. "It's the biggest challenge of your life."

The program begins with two weeks of training in Chicago, where students learn some of the basics behind studying dinosaurs. That way when students begin fieldwork, "they really understand what they're seeing," Barnes explained.

Then students take the train to Montana, where the real fun begins.

Students begin each day at 6 a.m. By 9 a.m. they head out to a field <u>site</u>, where they do everything from fossil collecting to digging for dinosaurs.

Gabrielle Lyon (left) and Susan, a Junior Paleontologist, apply a coating of plaster to a fossil found during fieldwork.

Students get right into the action. One of Barnes's favorite memories is the time a student found a dinosaur tooth that was 65 million years old.

"He was the first person to hold that particular tooth," Barnes said.

"I could not believe what I found," wrote one student, Marco, in his journal. "It was a tooth from a meat-eater . . . I yelled in happiness."

According to Barnes, "The <u>expedition</u> is just the beginning." Project Exploration continues to support the Junior

---

Vo·cab·u·lary

site (syt) the location of a dig
expedition (ek spi DISH un) a journey made for a specific purpose

Paleontologists when the program is over. Barnes said, "We want to spark and support the students' curiosity. We want them to be lifelong learners."

More about the Junior Paleontologist Program

The Junior Paleontologist program selects kids from Chicago's public schools who show curiosity but don't necessarily have

This fossil was discovered by a Junior Paleontologist at the program's field site in Montana.

good grades. The program is not open to the public. It's free of charge, so any student can participate, regardless of ability to pay. Students must be in 7th through 11th grade.

Project Exploration was co-founded by Paul Sereno, paleontologist and National Geographic explorer-in-residence. To learn more about the program, go to Project Exploration (on the National Geographic website). ○

Answering the BIG Question

As you do the following activities, consider the Big Question:
How can we become who we want to be?

WRITE TO LEARN Write a brief entry in your Learner's Notebook about how this selection influenced your ideas about careers. What type of career would you like to explore?

LITERATURE GROUPS Join two or three other students who have read this selection. Discuss what you know about fossil collecting and digging for dinosaurs. Would you be interested in participating in a program like the Junior Paleontologists? What would you hope to gain from the experience?

...and the judges are in agreement!

TODAY: KUNG-FU TOURNAMENT

T'alzia Kronah wins the Junior Acrobatic competition!

9.2 9.3 9.1

CLAPCLAPCLAPCLAPCLAPCLAP

And now, the Level Five/Six sparring competition! First up, Carlos Car-Dom versus Nazz Folix!

Congrats, T'alzia!

Thanks! Good luck out there!

Contestants, take your positions on the hoverdisks!

...all a belt is really good for...

...is holding up your pants!

Here you go, sir. I'm definitely not ready for this yet.

It's okay, kid. You see, it's not about the belts. In the end it's all about what you've learned. The belt might represent that for some, but it doesn't instantly equal knowledge and ability.

You need to practice and enjoy what you do first and foremost. The rest will come naturally.

And don't be so hard on yourself! Having a goal is good, but you shouldn't let it take over your life.

WRITE TO LEARN
Think of a goal you have that is important to you. In your Learner's Notebook, write about how you think the goal will help you become the person you want to be.

CATERPILLARS

by Brod Bagert

How do you feel when you see a caterpillar?

They came like <u>dewdrops</u> overnight
Eating every plant in sight,
Those nasty worms with legs that crawl
So creepy up the garden wall,
Green prickly fuzz to hurt and sting
Each <u>unsuspecting</u> living thing.
How I hate them! Oh, you know
I'd love to squish them with my toe.
But then I see past their <u>disguise</u>,
Someday they'll all be butterflies. **1** ○

> **1 Activating Prior Knowledge**
> What do you know about caterpillars?

Answering the BIG Question

As you do the following activities, consider the Big Question:
How can we become who we want to be?

WRITE TO LEARN Write a brief entry in your Learner's Notebook about your looking beyond an outside appearance to discover beauty. Who are some people in your own life that you might look at differently?

LITERATURE GROUPS Join two or three other students who have read "Caterpillars." Discuss the author's opinion of caterpillars. Look for words in the poem that show how the author feels.

Vo·cab·u·lary

dewdrops (DOO drawps) drops of morning dew
unsuspecting (un seh SPEK ting) trusting; not suspicious
disguise (dis GYZ) a means of changing appearance

The Girl Who Makes the Cymbals Bang

by X.J. Kennedy

Can a girl play the cymbals as well as a boy?

I'm the girl who makes the <u>cymbals</u> bang—
It used to be a boy
That got to play them in the past
Which always would annoy
Me quite a bit. Though I complained,

Vo•cab•u•lary

cymbals (SIM bulz) brass plates that produce a clashing tone

Our teacher Mister Cash
Said, "Sorry, girls don't have the strength
To come up with a crash." **1**

"Oh yeah?" said I. "Please give them here!"
And there and then, I slammed
Together those brass plates so hard
His <u>eardrums</u> traffic-jammed.

He gulped and gaped, and I could tell
His old ideas were bending—
So now me and my cymbals give
Each song a real smash ending. ○

1 Connecting
Have you ever been told that you can't do something because you are a girl or because you are a boy?

Answering the BIG Question

As you do the following activities, consider the Big Question:
How can we become who we want to be?

WRITE TO LEARN Write a brief response in your Learner's Notebook about the ideas expressed in "The Girl Who Makes the Cymbals Bang." What old ideas do you see in your life that may still need "bending"? Have you ever "bent" someone else's old ideas?

PARTNER TALK Meet with another student who has also read "The Girl Who Makes the Cymbals Bang." Discuss how you could relate to the girl in the poem.

Vo·cab·u·lary

eardrums (EER drumz) parts of the inner ear

The Race

by Jennifer Trujillo

Don't gallop past the surprise ending!

She rode a horse named Fina
when women didn't ride.
They <u>galloped</u> around the mountain,
her legs on Fina's side.

She let her hair down from its bun
and felt it whip and fly.
She laughed and sang and whooped out loud.
Up there she wasn't shy!

One day great-grandma found her out
and planned to stop it all.
But down in town they'd heard some news . . .
they told her of a call.

A call for the <u>caballeros</u>
from all the highs and lows
to race their fancy <u>caballos</u>
to try and win the rose.

Vo•cab•u•lary

galloped (GA lupt) rode fast
caballeros (kab ah YER ohz) Spanish for horseback riders
caballos (kuh BAH yohz) Spanish for horses

Abuela looked at Fina,
a twinkle in her eye.
Abuela said, "Let's enter!
This race deserves a try." **1**

At dawn she was the only girl,
but didn't even care.
She came to meet the challenge, and
her horse was waiting there.

They swept across the finish line
much faster than the rest.
She flung her hat without surprise;
she'd always done her best.

Fina shook her mane and stomped.
Abuela flashed a smile.
She sniffed the rose and trotted off
in caballera style! ○

1 Connecting
Who encourages
you to try new
and different
things?

Answering the
BIG Question

As you do the following activities, consider the Big Question:
How can we become who we want to be?

WRITE TO LEARN Write a brief response in your Learner's Notebook about how the poem influenced your thinking on gender stereotypes. Are there any stereotypes in your own life that are preventing you from becoming who you want to be?

PARTNER TALK Meet with another student who has also read "The Race." Discuss a time when girls were not allowed to ride horses. What are some other past restrictions on girls that are now lifted? What barriers do girls still need to break through?

A
Determined
Pair

by Sharon Robinson

Find out how Jackie Robinson showed strength of character as both an athlete and a soldier.

After graduating from high school in 1937, Dad attended Pasadena Junior College (PJC), where he continued to build his sports <u>legacy</u>. Two important people came into his life at this point: a sprinter named Jack Gordon, and a young preacher by the name of the Reverend Karl Downs. Jack and my dad shared a love of sports and developed a close friendship that lasted a lifetime. The minister earned the respect of Dad and his friends. They soon learned that they could trust him with their problems. The Reverend Downs helped guide my father into manhood.

Jackie Robinson at batting practice

At PJC, my father set a national junior college record in track by beating his brother Mack's broad jump record. One newspaper called my father the greatest base runner ever to play on a junior college baseball team. That same newspaper named Dad athlete of the year. His <u>exploits</u> on the football field added to the legend. The Pasadena Elks gave Dad a gold football and named him Most Valuable Player. Needless to say, the college scholarship offers piled in. Dad chose to continue his education at the University of California at Los Angeles (UCLA).

Vo•cab•u•lary

legacy (LEG uh see) something handed down
exploits (EKS ployts) daring or heroic acts

The summer before Dad attended UCLA was a tough one. His mother moved into a smaller house, at 133 Pepper Street, leaving the house at 121 Pepper Street to her grown children. That same year, Dad's brother Frank was tragically killed in a motorcycle accident. In spite of the personal loss, Dad started at UCLA in the fall of 1939. He commuted by car from Pasadena to UCLA, where he once again lettered in four sports. ❶

❶ **Understanding Sequence**
In what order is the author telling Robinson's story?

By senior year, he was named the best all-around athlete on the West Coast. He twice led the Pacific Coast Conference in basketball scoring, won the Pacific Coast Intercollegiate Golf Championship, and reached the National Negro Tennis Tournament semifinals. But, perhaps the most significant thing to happen to Dad that year was meeting Rachel Annetta Isum . . . my mom.

My parents met on UCLA's campus in the fall of 1940. Mom was an eager freshman just thrilled to be in college. Dad was a mighty senior, stunning athlete, and "big man on campus." Mom was attracted to Dad immediately. She liked his warm, engaging smile, and the fact that he was confident without being <u>cocky</u>.

In the 1940s, black students at UCLA were a very small minority. Each day between classes they gathered in Kerckhoff Hall to eat and talk. This is where my mother and father met frequently and then began to date.

My parents were serious people with strong personal goals. Each wanted to be somebody. Mom wanted to be the first in her family to earn a college degree. Dad wanted to be a professional athlete.

As the romance between my parents heated up, so did America's preparation for World War II (1939-1945). As African Americans protested against their <u>exclusion</u> from the growing

---

Vo·cab·u·lary

cocky (KAW kee) boldly self-confident
exclusion (ek SKLOO zhun) the act of being left out

defense industry, Dad proposed to my mom. Not long after President Franklin Delano Roosevelt signed an executive order banning discrimination in all plants working on national defense contracts, my father was drafted into the United States Army. It was still segregated.

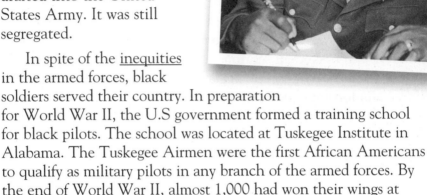

In spite of the <u>inequities</u> in the armed forces, black soldiers served their country. In preparation for World War II, the U.S government formed a training school for black pilots. The school was located at Tuskegee Institute in Alabama. The Tuskegee Airmen were the first African Americans to qualify as military pilots in any branch of the armed forces. By the end of World War II, almost 1,000 had won their wings at Tuskegee Army Airfield.

Dad was in the army for three years, from 1942 to 1944. Mom stayed at UCLA to get her degree. My parents were separated except for the times Dad came home on leave. My father wrote to Mom several times a week and sent a box of chocolates on Fridays. The separation was hard on both of them, but Mom believes that it helped prepare them for their life together.

Dad was <u>stationed</u> at Fort Riley, Kansas, and Fort Hood, Texas. Because of an old football injury, he wasn't sent overseas. Instead, he was assigned to the <u>cavalry</u>, where with the help of fellow soldier and boxing champion Joe Louis, he went to officers' training school and graduated as a second lieutenant.

Neither Dad's rank of second lieutenant nor his college athletic

Vo•cab•u•lary

inequities (in EK wih teez) instances of unfairness
stationed (STAY shund) assigned
cavalry (KAV el ree) army division on horseback

celebrity protected him against the humiliation of serving in a segregated army in the Deep South. Dad served as a morale officer, yet could do nothing about the fact that the baseball team was segregated, whereas the football team was not. One way he protested this injustice was by refusing to play any sport for the army.

Toward the end of his stint in the armed forces, my father faced Jim Crow[1] head on. During a bus ride from the army base into town, the bus driver ordered my father to the back of the bus, a section for black people only. Dad ignored the command; he knew his rights as a soldier. An argument followed, and Dad was arrested. Later, he had to defend himself in military court. The charges were dismissed. **2**

2 Inferring
What do you learn about Jackie Robinson's character from the way he dealt with segregation?

On November 28, 1944, Dad was honorably discharged from the army. A year later, America and her allies declared victory over Hitler. With the war over, attention turned to peace at home. ○

![icon] **Answering the**
BIG Question

As you do the following activities, consider the Big Question:
How can we become who we want to be?

WRITE TO LEARN In what areas today are people still discriminated against based on race or gender? Write a response in your Learner's Notebook.

PARTNER TALK Meet with another student who has also read this selection. Name two people who influenced Jackie Robinson. Discuss the people who have had an influence on your life.

. . . .

[1] The Jim Crow laws said public places were "separate but equal." They were the legal justification behind everything from separate bathrooms to separate train cars for blacks and whites, and were overturned by the Civil Rights Act of 1964.

THE dog DIARIES

by Merrill Markoe

"It's a dog's life" takes on new meaning for this author.

I pick dogs that remind me of myself—scrappy, mutt-faced, with a hint of mange. People look for a reflection of their own personalities or the person they dream of being in the eyes of an animal companion. That is the reason I sometimes look into the face of my dog Stan and see <u>wistful</u> sadness and <u>existential angst</u>, when all he is actually doing is slowly scanning the ceiling for flies.

We pet owners demand a great deal from our pets. When we give them the job, it's a career position. Pets are required to listen to us <u>blithely</u>, even if we talk to them in infantile and goofy tones

---

Vo•cab•u•lary

wistful (WIST ful) full of longing
existential angst (eg zis TEN shul ayngkst) worry about the meaning of one's life
blithely (BLYTH lee) in a happy, lighthearted way

of voice that we'd never dare use around another human being for fear of being forced into psychiatric observation. On top of that, we make them wear little sweaters or jackets, and not just the cool kind with the push-up sleeves, either, but weird little felt ones that say, *It's raining cats and dogs.*

We are pretty sure that we and our pets share the same reality, until one day we come home to find that our wistful, intelligent friend who reminds us of our better self has decided a good way to spend the day is to open a box of Brillo pads, unravel a few, distribute some throughout the house, and eat or wear all the rest. And we shake our heads in an inability to comprehend what went wrong here.

Is he bored or is he just out for revenge? He certainly can't be as stupid as this would indicate. In order to answer these questions more fully, I felt I needed some kind of new perspective, a perspective that comes from really knowing both sides of the story.

Thus, I made up my mind to live with my pets as one of them: to share their hopes, their fears, their squeaking vinyl lamb chops, their drinking space at the toilet.

What follows is the revealing, sometimes shocking, sometimes terrifying, sometimes really stupid diary that resulted. ❶

❶ inferring Does the narrator really want to become a dog?

8:45 A.M. We have been lying on our sides in the kitchen for almost an hour now. We started out in the bedroom with just our heads under the bed. But then one of us heard something, and we all ran to the back door. I think our quick response was rather effective because, although I never <u>ascertained</u> exactly what we heard to begin with, I also can't say I recall ever hearing it again.

9:00 A.M. We carefully inspected the molding in the hallway, which led us straight to the heating duct by the bedroom. Just a coincidence? None of us was really sure. So we watched it

---

Vo•cab•u•lary

ascertained (as ur TAYND) made certain; found out

suspiciously for a while. Then we watched it for a little while longer.

Then, never letting it out of our sight, we all took a nap. ❷

10:00 A.M. I don't really know whose idea it was to yank back the edge of the carpet and pull apart the carpet pad, but talk about a rousing good time! How strange that I could have lived in this house for all these years, and never before felt the fur of a carpet between my teeth. Or actually bit into a moist, chewy chunk of carpet padding. I will never again think of the carpet as simply a covering for the floor.

> ❷ **Understanding Sequence**
> What clues help you keep track of the order of events?

11:15 A.M. When we all wound up in the kitchen, the other two began to stare at me eagerly. Their meaning was clear. The pressure was on for me to produce snacks. They remembered the old me—the one with the <u>prehensile</u> thumb, the one who could open refrigerators and cabinets. I saw they didn't yet realize that today, I intended to live as their equal. But as they continued their staring, I soon became caught up in their obsession. That is the only explanation I have as to why I helped them topple over the garbage. At first I was nervous, watching the murky fluids soak into the floor. But the heady sense of acceptance I felt when we all dove headfirst into the can more than made up for my compromised sense of right and wrong. Pack etiquette demanded that I be the last in line. By the time I really got my head in there, the really good stuff was gone. But wait! I spied a tiny piece of tinfoil hidden in a giant clump of hair, and inside, a wad of previously chewed gum, lightly coated with sugar or salt. I was settling down to my treasure when I had the sense that I was being watched. Raising my head just slightly, I looked into the noses of my companions. Their eyes were glued to that hard rubber mass. Their drools were long and elastic, and so, succumbing to peer pressure, I split up my gum wad three ways.

Vo·cab·u·lary

prehensile (pree HEN sil) adapted for grasping

But I am not sure that I did the right thing. As is so often the case with wanting popularity, I may have gained their short-term acceptance. But I think that in the long run, I lost their real respect. No dog of reasonable intelligence would ever divide up something that could still be chewed.

11:50 A.M. Someone spotted a fly, and all three of us decided to catch him in our teeth. I was greatly relieved when one of the others got to him first.

12:20 P.M. Someone heard something, and in a flash, we were all in the backyard, running back and forth by the fence, periodically hooting. Then one of us spotted a larger-than-usual space between two of the fence boards, and using both teeth and nails, began to make the space larger. Pretty soon, all three of us were doing everything in our power to help. This was a case where the old prehensile thumb really came in handy. Grabbing hold of one of the splinters, I was able to enlarge the hole immediately. Ironically, I alone was unable to squeeze through to freedom, and so I watched with envy as the others ran in pointless circles in the lot next door. What was I going to do? All of my choices were difficult. Sure, I could go back into the house and get a hacksaw, or I could simply let myself out the back gate, but if I did that, did I not betray my companions? And would I not then be obligated to round us all up and punish us? No, I was a collaborator, and I had the lip splinters to prove it. So I went back to the hole and continued chewing. Only a few hundred dollars' worth of fence damage later, I was able to squeeze through that darn hole myself.

1:30 P.M. The extra time I took was just enough for me to lose sight of my two companions. And so, for the first time, I had to rely on my keen, new animal instincts. Like the wild creature I had become, I was able to spot their tracks immediately. They led me in a series of ever-widening circles, then across the lot at a forty-five-degree angle, then into a series of zigzags, then back to the hole again. Finally, I decided to abandon the tracking and head out to the sidewalk. Seconds later, I spotted them both across the street, where they were racing up and back in front of the neighbor's house. They seemed glad to see me, and so I eagerly joined them in their project. The three of us had only been running and hooting for less than an hour when the apparent owner of the house came to the front door. And while I admit this may not have been the best of circumstances for a first introduction, nevertheless I still feel the manner in which he threatened to turn the hose on us was both excessively violent and unnecessarily vulgar.

Clearly, it was up to me to encourage our group to relocate, and I was shocked at how easily I could still take command of our unit. A simple "Let's go, boys," and everyone was willing to follow me home. (It's such a power-packed phrase. That's how I met my last boyfriend!)

3:00 P.M. By the time we had moved our running and hooting activities into our own front yard, we were all getting a little tired. So we lay down on our sides on the porch.

4:10 P.M. We all changed sides.

4:45 P.M. We all changed sides again.

5:20 P.M. We all lay on our backs. (What a nice change of pace!)

6:00 P.M. Everyone was starting to grow restless. Occasionally, one of us would get up, scratch the front door, and moan. I wrestled silently with the temptation simply to let us all in. But then I realized I didn't have any keys on me. Of course, it occurred to me that we could all go back through the new hole in the fence, but everyone else seemed to have forgotten about the entire fence incident by this time. As they say, "a word to the wise." And so, taking a hint from my friends, I began to forget about the whole thing myself.

6:30 P.M. The sound of an approaching car as it pulls into the driveway. The man who shares this house with us is coming home. He is both surprised and perplexed to see us all out in the front yard running in circles. He is also quickly irritated by the fact that no one offers any explanations. And once he opens the front door, he unleashes a furious string of harsh words as he confronts the mounds of garbage someone has strewn all over the house. We have nothing but sympathy for him in his tragic misfortune. But since none of us knows anything about it, we all retire to the coat closet until the whole thing blows over. And later, as he eats his dinner, I sit quietly under the table. As I watch him, a pleasant feeling of calm overtakes me as I realize just how much I have grown as a person. Perhaps that is why the cruel things he says to me seem to have no effect. And so, when he gets up to pour himself another beverage, I raise my head up to his plate, and, with my teeth, I lift off his sandwich. **3** ○

> **3 Inferring**
> Who do you think this man is?

Answering the BIG Question

As you do the following activities, consider the Big Question:
How can we become who we want to be?

WRITE TO LEARN If dogs could provide answers, what questions would you have for them? Write a few questions for your pet or some other animal in your Learner's Notebook.

LITERATURE GROUPS Get together with two or three others who have read "The Dog Diaries." Discuss what the narrator learns about her dogs when she looks at life from their perspective.

IT'S NOT A CRIME TO LOVE SCIENCE

by Juliann F. Willey

Not enough girls taking science? It's a crime! Find out why.

"**C**hemistry class led me to a life of crime." This has become something of a personal <u>slogan</u>. I could also honestly, and perhaps more accurately, say that "Science class led me to a life of crime," because it was my interest in science as a child that planted the seeds for the job I have today: Director of the Delaware State Police Crime Lab, which means I supervise a team made up of a <u>forensic</u> microscopist (me), a questioned-document examiner, two chemists, and a photographer.

When I was a little girl, my love for animals made me think I would one day become a veterinarian. When I got the chance to participate in hands-on science classes and labs in junior high school, I knew for sure that I wanted to grow up to work in science.

Vo·cab·u·lary

slogan (SLOH gun) a brief, attention-getting phrase
forensic (fuh REN sik) relating to science and legal problems

I can remember dissecting earthworms, frogs, and starfish—and not thinking, Yuck!, but rather how cool it was to find out how these creatures functioned. I can remember learning about the planets and the stars so far up above and about minerals and fossils beneath the earth's surface and thinking, Wow! What a world!

My excitement over science did nothing but grow during high school and during my college days, too—only by then I had discovered that I didn't want to be a veterinarian. My courses in analytical and organic chemistry and biochemistry helped me understand how and why things worked the way they do—from how the chemicals in perms make your hair curly to why your blood clots when you get a cut or bruise. Eventually my focus became forensics—the application of science to matters of the law. My interest in forensics had actually been sparked a few years earlier by the television series *Quincy, M.E.*, which starred Jack Klugman as a feisty medical examiner who helped the Los Angeles County police department solve crimes.

Eventually I became a forensic microscopist, and with my three trusty Olympus microscopes I assist in crime-busting by analyzing what we call "known" items (like head hairs or clothing fibers from a victim) and "questioned" items (things collected at the scene of a crime, such as vacuum sweepings and suspects' clothing). The results of my examination are then handed over to the investigating officer—to be used in tracking down a criminal or proving the innocence of a suspect. ❶

❶ Understanding Sequence
What words and phrases help you to follow the order of events in the selection so far?

Given what I do for a living, when I spot something harmful, hurtful, and just plain wrong, I tend to view it as a crime. One of the crimes I've been scoping out for a while is the discouragement of girls from studying the sciences—a surefire method of scaring many away from ever at least considering a career in the field.

And it's a serial crime, taking place all across the nation, affecting girl after girl, day after day. When I contemplate what can be done about it, I can't help but fall back on the procedures I use in my work.

So I've looked at the "known" items—information found in various studies—which include:

- Girls are not being encouraged to take science class.

- Boys and girls are not being treated equally in many classrooms.

- Different expectations are placed on boys than on girls. **2**

2 Connecting Do these items agree with what you have observed?

As for the "questioned" items, traces of strange ideas have been found again and again at the scenes of the crime. Among them:

1. A person who loves science class is definitely uncool.

2. Having a passion for science will have you doing nothing but homework, with no time for fun.

3. The worst thing a girl can do is show her "mental muscles"—especially in front of boys.

4. Anyone who pursues a career in the sciences will end up in some boring job in some boring lab in some boring company somewhere.

My analysis strongly suggests that the prime suspects are Stereotypes and Ignorance, repeat offenders that have been around for a very long time, clogging girls' heads with a lot of nonsense, a lot of lies. They've even got some parents, teachers, and guidance counselors serving as their <u>accomplices</u>—sometimes willingly and often unwittingly—when, for example, they discourage girls from adventures in something like carpentry or auto mechanics. What's more, the culprits have operatives in the entertainment and advertising industries who put out the vile message that a female's sole purpose in life is to be beautiful.

What's to be done? I can't think of anything more necessary than a big dose of truth.

Vo·cab·u·lary

accomplices (uh KAWM plus ez) those associated with others in wrongdoing

1. There's nothing more uncool than letting other people keep you from the positive things you enjoy.

2. If you run across a science maniac who's all work and no play, trust me, it's a personality thing. It's not biology or chemistry class that has made this person antisocial and one-dimensional. I am living proof that you can be serious about science and have fun. In high school I ran varsity cross-country, played varsity basketball, participated in various clubs, and went out with friends.

3. The *worst* thing a girl can do is hide her mental muscles—in front of anyone! Not that you should show off your smarts, but it's foolish to camouflage it, because the kinds of people who are worth your while are the kinds of people who respect, admire, and rejoice at intelligence. Those who are intimidated by a smart girl are *definitely* bad news. In the long run, their insecurity will only pull you down and hold you back.

4. The range of jobs in the world of science is awesome. There is something in the field for all kinds of personalities and interests. Science class could lead to a life of healing (a doctor), a life of improving our eating (nutritionist), a life of <u>probing</u> and protecting our world (astronomer, geologist, zoologist, marine biologist, environmental scientist), and so many other careers. When it comes to a job in which a lab is the primary work site, the fact of the matter is that fascinating things go on in labs, and there's really little room for boredom. Think of the challenges facing our world today, such as finding cures for cancer, AIDS, and other diseases; creating vegetable plants that generate high-yield, robust produce; developing materials and

---

Vo•cab•u•lary

probing (PROH bing) searching and exploring thoroughly

products that are functional yet biodegradable. This is the kind of work that goes on in labs. Of course, if you're into justice and a safer nation, you could always become a forensic scientist like me.

Surely more teachers, parents, and other adults need to step up and join the science awareness patrol by, for example, buying a chemistry set as well as a tea set for a girl who's shown an interest and aptitude for science; by not making a girl feel that a life in the sciences is off-limits to her merely because she is female. **3**

3 Inferring
How should society's attitude toward girls change?

Such tactics have tremendous value, but it's also <u>vital</u> for girls to take preventive measures to avoid becoming a victim of the crime, by saying no to Stereotypes and Ignorance, by holding up the truth.

And the world will become a more welcoming place for girls who want to say yes to the sciences. ○

Answering the BIG Question

As you do the following activities, consider the Big Question:
How can we become who we want to be?

WRITE TO LEARN Have you encountered stereotypes about brainy girls or girls who like science? If you are a girl, how did they make you feel? If you are a boy, do you believe any of them? Write a response in your Learner's Notebook.

LITERATURE GROUPS Join two or three other students who have read this selection. Discuss one career in which you can foresee obstacles to success. What positive steps can be taken to overcome these obstacles?

Vo•cab•u•lary

vital (VY tul) very important

HOLLYWOOD and the PITS

by Cherylene Lee

Find out how a child actress made her way from the stage to the sticky brown La Brea Tar Pits.

In 1968 when I was fifteen, the pit opened its secret to me. I breathed, ate, slept, dreamed about the La Brea Tar Pits. I spent summer days working the <u>archaeological</u> dig and in dreams saw the bones glistening, the broken pelvises, the skulls, the vertebrae looped like a woman's pearls hanging on an invisible cord. I welcomed those dreams. I wanted to know where the next

Vo•cab•u•lary

archaeological (ar kee uh LAWJ ih kul) relating to the scientific study of prehistory by examining remains

skeleton was, identify it, record its position, discover whether it was whole or not. I wanted to know where to dig in the coarse, black, gooey sand. I lost myself there and found something else.

My mother thought something was wrong with me. Was it good for a teenager to be fascinated by death? Especially animal death in the <u>Pleistocene</u>? Was it normal to be so obsessed by a sticky brown hole in the ground in the center of Los Angeles? I don't know if it was normal or not, but it seemed perfectly logical to me. After all, I grew up in Hollywood, a place where dreams and nightmares can often take the same shape. What else would a child actor do?

"Thank you very much, dear. We'll be letting you know."

I knew what that meant. It meant I would never hear from them again. I didn't get the job. I heard that phrase a lot that year.

I walked out of the plush office, leaving behind the casting director, producer, director, writer, and whoever else came to listen to my reading for a semi-regular role on a family sit-com. The carpet made no sound when I opened and shut the door.

I passed the other girls waiting in the reception room, each poring over her script. The mothers were waiting in a separate room, chattering about their daughters' latest commercials, interviews, callbacks, jobs. It sounded like every Oriental kid in Hollywood was working except me.

My mother used to have a lot to say in those waiting rooms. Ever since I was three, when I started at the Meglin Kiddie Dance Studio, I was dubbed "The Chinese Shirley Temple"—always the one to be picked at auditions and interviews, always the one to get the speaking lines, always called "the one-shot kid," because I could do my scenes in one take—even tight close-ups. My mother would only talk about me behind my back because she didn't want me to hear her brag, but I knew that she was proud. In a

Vo•cab•u•lary

Pleistocene (PLYS tuh seen) a long period of time in the earth's history marked by periods of glaciers and recession; also called the Ice Age

way I was proud too, though I never dared admit it. I didn't want to be called a show-off. But I didn't exactly know what I did to be proud of either. I only knew that at fifteen I was now being passed over at all these interviews when before I would be chosen. My mother looked at my face hopefully when I came into the room. I gave her a quick shake of the head. She looked <u>bewildered</u>. I felt bad for my mother then. How could I explain it to her? I didn't understand it myself. We left saying polite good-byes to all the other mothers.

We didn't say anything until the studio parking lot, where we had to search for our old blue Chevy among rows and rows of parked cars baking in the Hollywood heat.

"How did it go? Did you read clearly? Did you tell them you're available?"

"I don't think they care if I'm available or not, Ma."

"Didn't you read well? Did you remember to look up so they could see your eyes? Did they ask you if you could play the piano? Did you tell them you could learn?"

The <u>barrage</u> of questions stopped when we finally spotted our car. I didn't answer her. My mother asked about the piano because I lost out in an audition once to a Chinese girl who already knew how to play.

My mother took off the towel that shielded the steering wheel from the heat. "You're getting to be such a big girl," she said, starting the car in neutral. "But don't worry, there's always next time. You have what it takes. That's special." She put the car into forward and we drove through a parking lot that had an endless number of identical cars all facing the same direction. We drove back home in silence.

I suppose a lot of my getting into show business in the first place was a matter of luck—being in the right place at the right

---

Vo•cab•u•lary

bewildered (bih WIL durd) confused
barrage (buh RAWZH) a rapid outpouring

Hollywood and the Pits

In the La Brea Tar Pits many of the excavated bones belong to juvenile mammals. Thousands of years ago thirsty young animals in the area were drawn to watering holes, not knowing they were traps. Those inviting pools had false bottoms made of sticky tar, which immobilized its victims and preserved their bones when they died. Innocence trapped by ignorance. The tar pits record that well. **1**

> **1 Inferring**
> How was Cherylene like the young mammals in the tar pits?

time. My sister, seven years older than me, was a member of the Meglin Kiddie Dance Studio long before I started lessons. Once during the annual recital held at the Shrine Auditorium, she was spotted by a Hollywood agent who handled only Oriental performers. The agent sent my sister out for a role in the CBS Playhouse 90 television show *The Family Nobody Wanted.* The producer said she was too tall for the part. But true to my mother's training of always having a positive reply, my sister said to the producer, "But I have a younger sister . . . " which started my show-biz career at the tender age of three.

My sister and I were lucky. We enjoyed singing and dancing, we were natural hams, and our parents never discouraged us. In fact, they were our biggest fans. My mother chauffeured us to all our dance lessons, lessons we begged to take. She drove us to interviews, took us to studios, went on location with us, drilled us on our lines, made sure we kept up our schoolwork and didn't sass back the tutors hired by studios to teach us for three hours a day. She never complained about being a stage mother. She said that we made her proud.

My father must have felt pride too, because he paid for a choreographer to put together our sister act: "The World Famous Lee Sisters," fifteen minutes of song and dance, real <u>vaudeville</u>

Vo•cab•u•lary

vaudeville (VAWD vil) describing a kind of entertainment consisting of various acts (dancers, singers, animal acts, jugglers, etc.)

stuff. We joked about that a lot, "Yeah, the Lee Sisters—Ug-Lee and Home-Lee," but we definitely had a good time. So did our parents. Our father especially liked our getting booked into Las Vegas at the New Frontier Hotel on the Strip. He liked to gamble there, though he said the craps tables in that hotel were "cold," not like the casinos in downtown Las Vegas, where all the "hot" action took place.

In Las Vegas our sister act was part of a show called "Oriental Holiday." The show was about a Hollywood producer going to the Far East, finding undiscovered talent, and bringing it back to the U.S. We did two shows a night in the main showroom, one at eight and one at twelve, and on weekends a third show at two in the morning. It ran the entire summer often to standing-room-only audiences—a thousand people a show.

Our sister act worked because of the age and height difference. My sister then was fourteen and nearly five foot two; I was seven and very small for my age—people thought we were cute. We had song and dance routines to old tunes like "Ma, He's Making Eyes at Me," "Together," and "I'm Following You," and my father hired a writer to adapt the lyrics to "I Enjoy Being a Girl," which came out "We Enjoy Being Chinese." We also told corny jokes, but the Las Vegas audience seemed to enjoy it. Here we were, two

The Lee sisters perform on Dinah Shore's TV show.

kids, staying up late and jumping around, and getting paid besides. To me the applause sometimes sounded like static, sometimes like distant waves. It always amazed me when people applauded. The owner of the hotel liked us so much, he invited us back to perform in shows for three summers in a row. That was before I grew too tall and the sister act didn't seem so cute anymore.

Many of the skeletons in the tar pits are found incomplete—particularly the skeletons of the young, which have only soft cartilage connecting the bones. In life the soft tissue allows for growth, but in death it dissolves quickly. Thus the skeletons of young animals are more apt to be scattered, especially the vertebrae protecting the spinal cord. In the tar pits, the central ends of many vertebrae are found unconnected to any skeleton. Such bone fragments are shaped like valentines, disks that are slightly lobed—heart-shaped shields that have lost their connection to what they were meant to protect.

I never felt my mother pushed me to do something I didn't want to do. But I always knew if something I did pleased her. She was generous with her praise, and I was sensitive when she withheld it. I didn't like to disappoint her.

I took to performing easily, and since I had started out so young, making movies or doing shows didn't feel like anything special. It was part of my childhood—like going to the dentist one morning or going to school the next. I didn't wonder if I wanted a particular role or wanted to be in a show or how I would feel if I didn't get in. Until I was fifteen, it never occurred to me that one day I wouldn't get parts or that I might not "have what it takes."

When I was younger, I got a lot of roles because I was so small for my age. When I was nine years old, I could pass for five or six. I was really short. I was always teased about it when I was in elementary school, but I didn't mind because my height got me movie jobs. I could read and memorize lines that actual five-year-olds couldn't. My mother told people she made me sleep in a drawer so I wouldn't grow any bigger.

But when I turned fifteen, it was as if my body, which hadn't grown for so many years, suddenly made up for lost time. I grew five inches in seven months. My mother was amazed. Even I couldn't get used to it. I kept knocking into things, my clothes didn't fit right, I felt awkward and clumsy when I moved. Dumb things that I had gotten away with, like paying children's prices at the movies instead of junior admission, I couldn't do anymore. I wasn't a shrimp or a small fry any longer. I was suddenly normal.

Before that summer my mother had always claimed she wanted me to be normal. She didn't want me to become spoiled by the attention I received when I was working at the studios. I still had chores to do at home, went to public school when I wasn't working, was punished severely when I behaved badly. She didn't want me to feel I was different just because I was in the movies. When I was eight, I was interviewed by a reporter who wanted to know if I thought I had a big head.

"Sure," I said.

"No, you don't," my mother interrupted, which was really unusual, because she generally never said anything. She wanted me to speak for myself.

I didn't understand the question. My sister had always made fun of my head. She said my body was too tiny for the weight—I looked like a walking Tootsie Pop. I thought the reporter was making the same observation.

"She better not get that way," my mother said fiercely. "She's not any different from anyone else. She's just lucky and small for her age."

The reporter turned to my mother, "Some parents push their children to act. The kids feel like they're used."

"I don't do that—I'm not that way," my mother told the reporter.

But when she was sitting silently in all those waiting rooms while I was being turned down for one job after another, I could almost feel her wanting to shout, "Use her. Use her. What is wrong with her? Doesn't she have it anymore?" I didn't know what I had had that I didn't seem to have anymore. My mother

Hollywood and the Pits

The churning action of the La Brea Tar Pits makes interpreting the record of past events extremely difficult. The usual order of <u>deposition</u>—the oldest on the bottom, the youngest on the top—loses all meaning when some of the oldest fossils can be brought to the surface by the movement of natural gas. One must look for an undisturbed spot, a place untouched by the action of underground springs or natural gas or human interference. Complete skeletons become important, because they indicate areas of least disturbance. But such spots of calm are rare. Whole blocks of the tar pit can become displaced, making false sequences of the past, <u>skewing</u> the interpretation for what is the true order of nature.

had told the reporter that I was like everyone else. But when my life was like everyone else's, why was she disappointed?

That year before my sixteenth birthday, my mother seemed to spend a lot of time looking through my old scrapbooks, staring at all the eight-by-ten glossies of the shows that I had done. In the summer we visited with my grandmother often, since I wasn't working and had lots of free time. I would go out to the garden to read or sunbathe, but I could hear my mother and grandmother talking. ❷

"She was so cute back then. She worked with Gene Kelly when she was five years old. She was so smart for her age. I don't know what's wrong with her."

"She's fifteen."

"She's too young to be an <u>ingenue</u> and too old to be cute. The studios forget so quickly. By the time she's old enough to play an ingenue, they won't remember her."

"Does she have to work in the movies? Hand me the scissors."

My grandmother was making false eyelashes using the hair

> **❷ Connecting**
> In what ways are Cherylene's upbringing and yours similar and different?

Vo·cab·u·lary

deposition (dep eh ZIH shun) the process in which soil is laid down
skewing (SKYOO ing) distorting or slanting
ingenue (AN juh noo) an innocent young woman

from her hairbrush. When she was young she had incredible hair. I saw an old photograph of her when it flowed beyond her waist like a cascading black waterfall. At seventy, her hair was still black as night, which made her few strands of silver look like shooting stars. But her hair had thinned greatly with age. It sometimes fell out in clumps.

She wore it brushed back in a bun with a hairpiece for added fullness. My grandmother had always been proud of her hair, but once she started making false eyelashes from it, she wasn't proud of the way it looked anymore. She said she was proud of it now because it made her useful.

It was painstaking work—tying knots into strands of hair, then tying them together to form feathery little crescents. Her glamorous false eyelashes were much sought after. Theatrical make-up artists waited months for her work. But my grandmother said what she liked was that she was doing something, making a contribution, and besides it didn't cost her anything. No overhead. "Till I go bald," she often joked.

She tried to teach me her art that summer, but for some reason strands of my hair wouldn't stay tied in knots.

"Too springy," my grandmother said. "Your hair is still too young." And because I was frustrated then, frustrated with everything about my life, she added, "You have to wait until your hair falls out, like mine. Something to look forward to, eh!" She had laughed and patted my hand.

My mother was going on and on about my lack of work, what might be wrong, that something she couldn't quite put her finger on. I heard my grandmother reply, but I didn't catch it all: "Movies are just make-believe, not real life. Like what I make with my hair that falls out—false. False eyelashes. Not meant to last."

I spent a lot of time by myself that summer, wondering what it was that I didn't have anymore. Could I get it back? How could I if I didn't know what it was?

That's when I discovered the La Brea Tar Pits. Hidden behind the County Art Museum on trendy Wilshire Boulevard, I found a

The remains in the La Brea Tar Pits are mostly of carnivorous animals. Very few herbivores are found—the ratio is five to one, a perversion of the natural food chain. The ratio is easy to explain. Thousands of years ago a thirsty animal sought a drink from the pools of water only to find itself trapped by the bottom, gooey with subterranean oil. A shriek of agony from the trapped victim drew flesh-eating predators, which were then trapped themselves by the very same ooze which provided the bait. The cycle repeated itself countless times. The number of victims grew, lured by the image of easy food, the deception of an easy kill. The animals piled on top of one another. For over ten thousand years the promise of the place drew animals of all sorts, mostly predators and <u>scavengers</u>—dire wolves, panthers, coyotes, vultures—all hungry for their chance. Most were sucked down against their will in those watering holes destined to be called the La Brea Tar Pits in a place to be named the City of Angels, home of Hollywood movie stars.

Vo•cab•u•lary

scavengers (SKAV en jurz) animals that feed on dead flesh

job that didn't require me to be small or cute for my age. I didn't have to audition. No one said, "Thank you very much, we'll call you." Or if they did, they meant it. I volunteered my time one afternoon, and my fascination stuck—like tar on the bones of a saber-toothed tiger.

My mother didn't understand what had changed me. I didn't understand it myself. But I liked going to the La Brea Tar Pits. It meant I could get really messy and I was doing it with a purpose. I didn't feel awkward there. I could wear old stained pants. I could wear T-shirts with holes in them. I could wear disgustingly filthy sneakers and it was all perfectly justified. It wasn't a costume for a role in a film or a part in a TV sit-com. My mother didn't mind my dressing like that when she knew I was off to the pits. That was okay so long as I didn't track tar back into the house. I started going to the pits every day, and my mother wondered why. She couldn't believe I would rather be groveling in tar than going on auditions or interviews. **3**

3 Inferring
What does Cherylene learn about herself in the tar pits?

While my mother wasn't proud of the La Brea Tar Pits (she didn't know or care what a fossil was), she didn't discourage me either. She drove me there, the same way she used to drive me to the studios.

"Wouldn't you rather be doing a show in Las Vegas than scrambling around in a pit?" she asked.

"I'm not in a show in Las Vegas, Ma. The Lee Sisters are retired." My older sister had married and was starting a family of her own.

"But if you could choose between. . ."

"There isn't a choice."

"You really like this tar-pit stuff, or are you just waiting until you can get real work in the movies?"

I didn't answer.

At the La Brea Tar Pits, everything dug out of the pit is saved—including the sticky sand that covered the bones through the ages. Each bucket of sand is washed, sieved, and examined for pollen grains, insect remains, any evidence of past life. Even the grain size is recorded—the percentage of silt to sand to gravel that reveals the history of deposition, erosion, and disturbance. No single fossil, no one observation, is significant enough to tell the entire story. All the evidence must be weighed before a <u>semblance</u> of truth emerges.

My mother sighed. "You could do it if you wanted, if you really wanted. You still have what it takes."

I didn't know about that. But then, I couldn't explain what drew me to the tar pits either. Maybe it was the bones, finding out what they were, which animal they belonged to, imagining how they got

---

Vo•cab•u•lary

semblance (SEM blans) outward appearance

there, how they fell into the trap. I wondered about that a lot.

The tar pits had its lessons. I was learning I had to work slowly, become observant, to concentrate. I learned about time in a way that I would never experience—not in hours, days, and months, but in thousands and thousands of years. I imagined what the past must have been like, envisioned Los Angeles as a sweeping basin, perhaps slightly colder and more humid, a time before people and studios arrived. The tar pits recorded a warming trend; the kinds of animals found there reflected the changing climate. The ones unadapted disappeared. No trace of their kind was found in the area. The ones adapted to warmer weather left a record of bones in the pit. Amid that collection of ancient skeletons, surrounded by evidence of death, I was finding a secret preserved over thousands and thousands of years. There was something cruel about natural selection and the survival of the fittest. Even those successful individuals that "had what it took" for adaptation still wound up in the pits.

I never found out if I had what it took, not the way my mother meant. But I did adapt to the truth: I wasn't a Chinese Shirley Temple any longer, cute and short for my age. I had grown up. Maybe not on a Hollywood movie set, but in the La Brea Tar Pits. ○

Answering the BIG Question

As you do the following activities, consider the Big Question:
How can we become who we want to be?

WRITE TO LEARN Think about childhood stars you know of. Have any of them been successful in Hollywood as adults? Is sacrificing your childhood worth this early career success? Write your ideas in your Learner's Notebook.

LITERATURE GROUPS Join two or three other students who have read "Hollywood and the Pits." Discuss the connection Cherylene Lee makes between digging in the La Brea Tar Pits and her career as a child performer. What does she learn about Hollywood from her work in the tar pits?

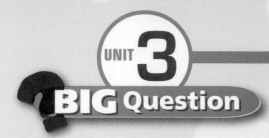

Who can we really count on?

As you read the following selections, you'll discover a variety of ways in which to think about the question: **Who can we really count on?** Some of the situations and characters may help you come up with your own answer to that question.

Key Reading Skills

As you read the selections in
this unit, apply these reading
skills.

- **Drawing Conclusions** Use
  evidence from what you read
  to make a general statement
  about people, events, places,
  and ideas.
- **Responding** React to what
  you read.
- **Synthesizing** Combine ideas
  to create something new.
- **Determining Main Idea/
  Supporting Details** Find the
  most important point or idea.

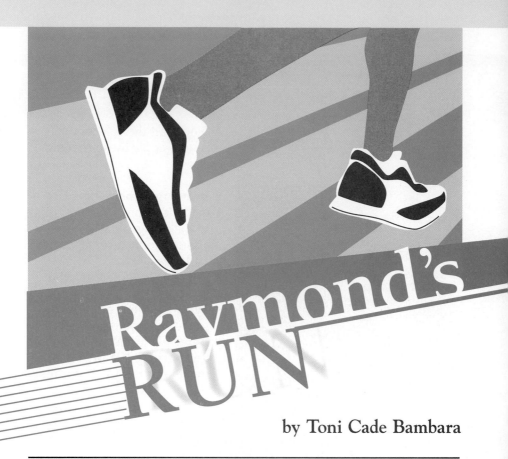

Raymond's RUN

by Toni Cade Bambara

A fifty-yard dash becomes more than a race to the finish line.

I don't have much work to do around the house like some girls. My mother does that. And I don't have to earn my pocket money by hustling; George runs errands for the big boys and sells Christmas cards. And anything else that's got to get done, my father does. All I have to do in life is mind my brother Raymond, which is enough.

Sometimes I slip and say my little brother Raymond. But as any fool can see he's much bigger and he's older too. But a lot of people call him my little brother 'cause he needs looking after 'cause he's not quite right. And a lot of smart mouths got lots to say about that too, especially when George was minding him. But now, if anybody has anything to say to Raymond, anything to say about his big head, they have to come by me. And I don't play the dozens[1] or believe in standing around with somebody in my face doing a lot of talking. I much rather just knock you down and take my chances even if I am a little girl with skinny arms and a squeaky voice, which is how I got the name Squeaky. And if things get too rough, I run. And as anybody can tell you, I'm the fastest thing on two feet.

There is no track meet that I don't win the first-place medal. I used to win the twenty-yard dash when I was a little kid in kindergarten. Nowadays, it's the fifty-yard dash. And tomorrow I'm subject to run the quarter-meter relay all by myself and come in first, second, and third. The big kids call me Mercury 'cause I'm the swiftest thing in the neighborhood. **1** Everybody knows that—except two people who know better, my father and me. He can beat me to Amsterdam Avenue with me having a two fire-hydrant head start and him running with his hands in his pockets and whistling. But that's private information. 'Cause can you imagine some thirty-five-year-old man stuffing himself into PAL shorts to race little kids? So as far as everyone's concerned, I'm the fastest and that goes for Gretchen, too, who has put out the tale that she is going to win the first-place medal this year. Ridiculous. In the second place, she's got short legs. In the third place, she's got freckles. In the first place, no one can beat me and that's all there is to it.

1 Responding What do you think of Squeaky's brag?

I'm standing on the corner admiring the weather and about to take a stroll down Broadway so I can practice my breathing exercises, and I've got Raymond walking on the inside close to the buildings, 'cause he's subject to fits of fantasy and starts thinking he's a circus performer and that the curb is a tightrope strung high in the air. And sometimes after a rain he likes to step down off his tightrope right into the gutter and slosh around getting his shoes and cuffs wet. Then I get hit when I get home. Or sometimes if you don't watch him he'll dash across traffic to the island in the middle of Broadway and give the pigeons a fit.

. . . .

[1] To *play the dozens* means to exchange insulting remarks.

Then I have to go behind him apologizing to all the old people sitting around trying to get some sun and getting all upset with the pigeons <u>fluttering</u> around them, scattering their newspapers and upsetting the wax paper lunches in their laps. So I keep Raymond on the inside of me, and he plays like he's driving a stage coach, which is O.K. by me so long as he doesn't run me over or interrupt my breathing exercises, which I have to do on account of I'm serious about my running, and I don't care who knows it.

Now some people like to act like things come easy to them, won't let on that they practice. Not me. I'll high-<u>prance</u> down 34th Street like a rodeo pony to keep my knees strong even if it does get my mother uptight so that she walks ahead like she's not with me, don't know me, is all by herself on a shopping trip, and I am somebody else's crazy child. Now you take Cynthia Procter for instance. She's just the opposite. If there's a test tomorrow, she'll say something like, "Oh, I guess I'll play handball this afternoon and watch television tonight," just to let you know she ain't thinking about the test. Or like last week when she won the spelling bee for the millionth time, "A good thing you got 'receive,' Squeaky, 'cause I would have got it wrong. I completely forgot about the spelling bee." And she'll clutch the lace on her blouse like it was a narrow escape. Oh, brother. ❷ But of course when I pass her house on my early morning trots around the block, she is practicing the scales on the piano over and over and over and over. Then in music class she always lets herself get bumped around so she falls accidentally on purpose onto the piano stool and is so surprised to find herself sitting there that she decides just for fun to try out the ole keys. And what do you know—Chopin's waltzes just spring out of her fingertips and she's the most surprised thing in the world. A regular <u>prodigy</u>. I could kill people like that. I stay up all

> ❷ **Drawing Conclusions**
> What does Squeaky think of Cynthia Procter?

Vo•cab•u•lary

fluttering (FLUH ter ing) flapping wings rapidly
prance (prans) to move like a horse rising up on its hind legs; to strut
prodigy (PRAH deh jee) an unusually talented child or person

night studying the words for the spelling bee. And you can see me any time of day practicing running. I never walk if I can trot, and shame on Raymond if he can't keep up. But of course he does, 'cause if he hangs back someone's <u>liable</u> to walk up to him and get smart, or take his allowance from him, or ask him where he got that great big pumpkin head. People are so stupid sometimes.

So I'm strolling down Broadway breathing out and breathing in on counts of seven, which is my lucky number, and here comes Gretchen and her sidekicks: Mary Louise, who used to be a friend of mine when she first moved to Harlem from Baltimore and got beat up by everybody till I took up for her on account of her mother and my mother used to sing in the same choir when they were young girls, but people ain't grateful, ❸ so now she hangs out with the new girl Gretchen and talks about me like a dog; and Rosie, who is as fat as I am skinny and has a big mouth where Raymond is concerned and is too stupid to know that there is not a big deal of difference between herself and Raymond and that she can't afford to throw stones. So they are steady coming up Broadway and I see right away that it's going to be one of those Dodge City scenes 'cause the street ain't that big and they're close to the buildings just as we are. First I think I'll step into the candy store and look over the new comics and let them pass. But that's chicken and I've got a reputation to consider. So then I think I'll just walk straight on through them and even over them if necessary. But as they get to me, they slow down. I'm ready to fight, cause like I said I don't <u>feature</u> a whole lot of chit-chat. I much prefer to just knock you down right from the jump and save everybody a lotta precious time.

❸ Drawing Conclusions
What conclusion can you draw about Squeaky's experiences with people when she says, "people ain't grateful"?

Vo•cab•u•lary

liable (LY uh bul) likely to do something unpleasant
feature (FEE chur) care for

"You signing up for the May Day races?" smiles Mary Louise, only it's not a smile at all. A dumb question like that doesn't deserve an answer. Besides, there's just me and Gretchen standing there really, so no use wasting my breath talking to shadows.

"I don't think you're going to win this time," says Rosie, trying to <u>signify</u> with her hands on her hips all salty, completely forgetting that I have whupped her behind many times for less salt than that.

"I always win 'cause I'm the best," I say straight at Gretchen who is, as far as I'm concerned, the only one talking in this ventriloquist-dummy routine. Gretchen smiles, but it's not a smile, and I'm thinking that girls never really smile at each other because they don't know how and don't want to know how and there's probably no one to teach us how, cause grown-up girls don't know either. Then they all look at Raymond who has just brought his mule team to a standstill. And they're about to see what trouble they can get into through him.

"What grade you in now, Raymond?"

"You got anything to say to my brother, you say it to me, Mary Louise Williams of Raggedy Town, Baltimore."

"What are you, his mother?" sasses Rosie.

"That's right, Fatso. And the next word out of anybody and I'll be their mother too." **❹** So they just stand there and Gretchen shifts from one leg to the other and so do they. Then Gretchen puts her hands on her hips and is about to say something with her freckle-face self but doesn't. Then she walks around me, looking me up and down, but keeps walking up Broadway, and her sidekicks follow her. So me and Raymond smile at each other and he says "Gidyap" to his team and I continue with my breathing

> **❹ Determining Main Idea/ Supporting Details**
> How does Squeaky feel about her responsibility for Raymond?

Vo•cab•u•lary

signify (SIG neh fy) to show or make known, often by a sign; to insult

exercises, strolling down Broadway toward the ice man on 145th with not a care in the world 'cause I am Miss <u>Quicksilver</u> herself.

I take my time getting to the park on May Day because the track meet is the last thing on the program. The biggest thing on the program is the May Pole dancing, which I can do without, thank you, even if my mother thinks it's a shame I don't take part and act like a girl for a change. You'd think my mother'd be grateful not to have to make me a white organdy dress with a big satin sash and buy me new white baby-doll shoes that can't be taken out of the box till the big day. You'd think she'd be glad her daughter ain't out there prancing around a May Pole getting the new clothes all dirty and sweaty and trying to act like a fairy or a flower or whatever you're supposed to be when you should be trying to be yourself, whatever that is, which is, as far as I am concerned, a poor Black girl who really can't afford to buy shoes and a new dress you only wear once a lifetime 'cause it won't fit next year.

I was once a strawberry in a Hansel and Gretel pageant when I was in nursery school and didn't have no better sense than to dance on tiptoe with my arms in a circle over my head doing umbrella steps and being a perfect fool just so my mother and father could come dressed up and clap. You'd think they'd know better than to encourage that kind of nonsense. I am not

---

Vo•cab•u•lary

quicksilver (KWIK sil vuhr) suggests mercury, a liquid metal that flows rapidly

a strawberry. I do not dance on my toes. I run. That is what I am all about. So I always come late to the May Day program, just in time to get my number pinned on and lie in the grass till they announce the fifty-yard dash.

I put Raymond in the little swings, which is a tight squeeze this year and will be impossible next year. Then I look around for Mr. Pearson, who pins the numbers on. I'm really looking for Gretchen if you want to know the truth, but she's not around. The park is jam-packed. Parents in hats and corsages and breast-pocket handkerchiefs peeking up. Kids in white dresses and light-blue suits. The parkees unfolding chairs chasing the rowdy kids from Lenox as if they had no right to be there. The big guys with their caps on backwards, leaning against the fence swirling the basketballs on the tips of their fingers, waiting for all these crazy people to clear out the park so they can play. Most of the kids in my class are carrying bass drums and <u>glockenspiels</u> and flutes. You'd think they'd put in a few bongos or something for real like that.

Then here comes Mr. Pearson with his clipboard and his cards and pencils and whistles and safety pins and fifty million other things he's always dropping all over the place with his clumsy self. He sticks out in a crowd because he's on stilts. We used to call him Jack and the Beanstalk to get him mad. But I'm the only one that can outrun him and get away, and I'm too grown for that silliness now.

"Well, Squeaky," he says checking my name off the list and handing me number seven and two pins. And I'm thinking he's got no right to call me Squeaky, if I can't call him Beanstalk.

"Hazel Elizabeth Deborah Parker," I correct him and tell him to write it down on his board.

"Well, Hazel Elizabeth Deborah Parker, going to give someone else a break this year?" I squint at him real hard to see if he is

---

Vo•cab•u•lary

glockenspiels (GLAH kehn speelz) musical instruments you strike with small hammers

seriously thinking I should lose the race on purpose just to give someone else a break. "Only six girls running this time," he continues, shaking his head sadly like it's my fault all of New York didn't turn out in sneakers. "That new girl should give you a run for your money." He looks around the park for Gretchen like a <u>periscope</u> in a submarine movie. "Wouldn't it be a nice gesture if you were. . . to ahhh. . ."

I give him such a look he couldn't finish putting that idea into words. Grownups got a lot of nerve sometimes. I pin number seven to myself and stomp away, I'm so burnt. **5** And I go straight for the track and stretch out on the grass while the band winds up with "Oh, the Monkey Wrapped His Tail Around the Flag Pole," which my teacher calls by some other name. The man on the loudspeaker is calling everyone over to the track and I'm on my back looking at the sky, trying to pretend I'm in the country, but I can't, because even grass in the city field feels hard as sidewalks, and there's just no pretending you are anywhere but in a "concrete jungle" as my grandfather says.

5 Responding How do Squeaky and "the Beanstalk" clash?

The twenty-yard dash takes all of two minutes 'cause most of the little kids don't know no better than to run off the track or run the wrong way or run smack into the fence and fall down and cry. One little kid, though, has got the good sense to run straight for the white ribbon up ahead so he wins. Then the second-graders line up for the thirty-yard dash and I don't even bother to turn my head to watch 'cause Raphael Perez always wins. He wins before he even begins by psyching the runners, telling them they're going to trip on their shoelaces and fall on their faces or lose their shorts or something, which he doesn't really have to do since he is very fast, almost as fast as I am. After that is the forty-yard dash which I used to run when I was in first grade. Raymond

Vo•cab•u•lary

periscope (PEHR eh skope) a type of lens with an eyepiece and a long tube used in submarines

is hollering from the swings 'cause he knows I'm about to do my thing 'cause the man on the loudspeaker has just announced the fifty-yard dash, although he might just as well be giving a recipe for angel food cake 'cause you can hardly make out what he's saying for the static. I get up and slip off my sweat pants and then I see Gretchen standing at the starting line, kicking her legs out like a pro. Then as I get into place I see that ole Raymond is on line on the other side of the fence, bending down with his fingers on the ground just like he knew what he was doing. I was going to yell at him but then I didn't. It burns up your energy to holler.

Every time, just before I take off in a race, I always feel like I'm in a dream, the kind of dream you have when you're sick with fever and feel all hot and weightless. I dream I'm flying over a sandy beach in the early morning sun, kissing the leaves of the trees as I fly by. And there's always the smell of apples, just like in the country when I was little and used to think I was a choo-choo train, running through the fields of corn and chugging up the hill to the orchard. And all the time I'm dreaming this, I get lighter and lighter until I'm flying over the beach again, getting blown through the sky like a feather that weighs nothing at all. ❻ But once I spread my fingers in the dirt and crouch over the Get on Your Mark, the dream goes and I am solid again and am telling myself, Squeaky, you must win, you must win, you are the fastest thing in the world, you can even beat your father up Amsterdam if you really try. And then I feel my weight coming back just behind my knees then down to my feet then into the earth and the pistol shot explodes in my blood and I am off and weightless again, flying past the other runners, my arms pumping up and down and the whole world is quiet except for the crunch as I zoom over the gravel in the track. I glance to my left and there is no one. To the right, a blurred Gretchen, who's got her chin jutting out as if it would win the race all by itself. And on the other side of the fence is Raymond with his arms down to his side and his palms tucked up behind him, running in his very own style, and it's the first time I ever saw that and I almost stop to watch my brother Raymond

> ❻ **Determining Main Idea**
> How does Squeaky prepare for the race?

on his first run. But the white ribbon is bouncing toward me and I tear past it, racing into the distance till my feet with a mind of their own start digging up footfuls of dirt and brake me short. Then all the kids standing on the side pile on me, banging me on the back and slapping my head with their May Day programs, for I have won again and everybody on 151st Street can walk tall for another year.

"In the first place . . ." the man on the loudspeaker is clear as a bell now. But then he pauses and the loudspeaker starts to whine. Then static. And I lean down to catch my breath and here comes Gretchen walking back, for she's overshot the finish line too, huffing and puffing with her hands on her hips taking it slow, breathing in steady time like a real pro, and I sort of like her a little for the first time. "In first place . . ." and then three or four voices get all mixed up on the loudspeaker and I dig my sneaker into the grass and stare at Gretchen who's staring back, we both wondering just who did win. I can hear old Beanstalk arguing with the man on the loudspeaker and then a few others running their mouths about what the stopwatches say. Then I hear Raymond yanking at the fence to call me and I wave to shush him, but he keeps rattling the fence like a gorilla in a cage like in them gorilla movies, but then like a dancer or something he starts climbing up nice and easy but very fast. And it occurs to me, watching how smoothly he climbs hand over hand and remembering how he looked running with his arms down to his side and with the wind pulling his mouth back and his teeth showing and all, it occurred to me that Raymond would make a very fine runner. Doesn't he always keep up with me on my trots? And he surely knows how to breathe in counts of seven 'cause he's always doing it at the dinner table, which drives my brother George up the wall. And I'm smiling to beat the band 'cause if I've lost this race, or if me and Gretchen tied, or even if I've won, I can always retire as a runner and begin a whole new career as a coach with Raymond as my champion. After all, with a little more study I can beat Cynthia and her phony self at the spelling bee. And if I bugged my mother, I could get piano lessons and become a star. And I have a big rep as the baddest thing around. And I've got a roomful of ribbons and medals and awards. But what has Raymond got to call his own?

So I stand there with my new plans, laughing out loud by this time as Raymond jumps down from the fence and runs over with his teeth showing and his arms down to the side, which no one before him has quite mastered as a running style. And by the time he comes over I'm jumping up and down so glad to see him—my brother Raymond, a great runner in the family tradition. But of course everyone thinks I'm jumping up and down because the men on the loudspeaker have finally gotten themselves together and compared notes and are announcing, "In first place—Miss Hazel Elizabeth Deborah Parker." (Dig that.) "In second place—Miss Gretchen P. Lewis." And I look over at Gretchen wondering what the "P" stands for. And I smile. Cause she's good, no doubt about it. Maybe she'd like to help me coach Raymond; she obviously is serious about running, as any fool can see. And she nods to congratulate me and then she smiles. And I smile. We stand there with this big smile of respect between us. It's about as real a smile as girls can do for each other, considering we don't practice real smiling every day, you know, 'cause maybe we too busy being flowers or fairies or strawberries instead of something honest and worthy of respect . . . you know . . . like being people. **7** ○

> **7 Synthesizing**
> What makes Squeaky change her mind about Gretchen?

Answering the BIG Question

When you do the following activities, consider the Big Question:
Who can we really count on?

WRITE TO LEARN Recall a time when you defended someone or could have defended someone who was being ridiculed by others. Make an entry in your Learner's Notebook about this experience. Explain why you acted on behalf of another or why you remained silent.

LITERATURE GROUPS Meet with two or three students who have read this story. Discuss how the author has influenced your way of thinking about friendship.

Tales of a Seventh Grade NADA

by Bizet Kizcorn

Find out who Kara can really count on.

If only I could come up with comebacks like these, Laura would stop making fun of me.

Maria said that I wasn't a total dork. I just hang out with nerds too much.

"Shut up, Laura!"

No. Too stupid.

"Everyone thinks you're mean, Laura."

What am I, a baby?

Sara, you talk so much your telephone melted!

Wait! I can just write these down!

Montel, your mouth is so big Batman thought it was his cave!

Perfect!

This one is totally you.

It's kind of naughty schoolgirl, but with a hint of sophistication.

Here.

Take it home and study it.

Naughty schoolgirl?

And take this back.

But I bought it for you.

It's a classic.

One of my favorite...

This is for kids.

It's fun if you're a kid. But this is not part of the project.

I'll bet she didn't even read one page!

But it's NOT just for kids, it's— what project?

YOU, dummy. Taking an ugly duckling and helping her become a swan.

A swan? She thinks I'm a project?

Now, NO more kids' stuff.

You're a woman now. Strength. Savvy. Solid thinking.

WRITE TO LEARN
A graphic novel tells a story in comic format. Each scene is called a "cell." Write a scene (or two) that illustrates what Kara finds out about herself and her friends. Include dialogue.

Lou Gehrig:
The Luckiest Man on the Face of the Earth

New York City, July 4, 1939

The legendary New York Yankee Lou Gehrig was forced to quit baseball in May of 1939 due to a rare disease. He spoke to a full house at Yankee Stadium on Lou Gehrig Day that July.

Fans, for the past two weeks you have been reading about a bad break I got. Yet today I consider myself the luckiest man on the face of the earth. I have been in ballparks for seventeen years and have never received anything but kindness and encouragement from you fans. ❶

Look at these grand men. Which of you wouldn't consider it the highlight of his career just to associate with them for even one day?

Sure, I'm lucky. Who wouldn't consider it an honor to have known Jacob Ruppert; also the builder of baseball's greatest empire, Ed Barrow; to have spent six years with that wonderful little fellow Miller Huggins; then

> ❶ **Determining Main Idea/ Supporting Details**
> Why is Lou Gehrig grateful?

to have spent the next nine years with that outstanding leader, that smart student of <u>psychology</u>—the best manager in baseball today—Joe McCarthy!

Sure, I'm lucky. When the New York Giants, a team you would give your right arm to beat, and vice versa, sends you a gift, that's something! When everybody down to the groundskeepers and those boys in white coats remember you with trophies, that's something.

When you have a wonderful mother-in-law who takes sides with you in <u>squabbles</u> against her own daughter, that's something. When you have a father and mother who work all their lives so that you can have an education and build your body, it's a blessing! When you have a wife who has been a tower of strength and shown more courage than you dreamed existed, that's the finest I know.

So I close in saying that I might have had a tough break; but I have an awful lot to live for! ○

Answering the BIG Question

When you do the following activities, consider the Big Question:
Who can we really count on?

WRITE TO LEARN Who were the people in Lou Gehrig's life that he could count on? Who were some of the people who could count on him? Write your responses in your Learner's Notebook.

PARTNER TALK Meet with another student who has read Lou Gehrig's speech. Discuss how Lou Gehrig handled the news of his illness and his forced retirement from baseball, a sport he loved. What might he have been feeling? What character traits made Lou Gehrig a great man as well as a great ballplayer?

Vo•cab•u•lary

psychology (sy KAWL eh jee) the study of the emotional and behavioral characteristics of a person or group
squabbles (SKWAB ulz) minor disagreements

Through these poems, you will meet different people who can be counted on.

TO LOU GEHRIG

by John Kieran

"To Lou Gehrig" is a tribute to one of the most talented baseball players of all time.

We've been to the wars together;
We took our foes as they came;
And always you were the leader,
And ever you played the game.

Idol of cheering millions,
Records are yours by <u>sheaves</u>;
Iron of frame they hailed you,
Decked you with <u>laurel</u> leaves.
But higher than that we hold you,
We who have known you best,
Knowing the way you came through
Every human test.

Let this be a silent <u>token</u>
Of lasting friendship's gleam
And all that we've left unspoken—
Your pals of the Yankee team.

Vo·cab·u·lary

sheaves (sheevz) bundles of items, as in papers
laurel (LOR el) leaves from trees often woven into wreaths; used by ancient Greeks to crown winners
token (TOH ken) a sign or symbol of something

A SONG FOR MAMA

by Boyz II Men

You may be surprised to discover who Boyz II Men can count on.

You taught me everything and everything you've given me
I always keep it inside
You're the driving force in my life, ey, yeah
There isn't anything or anyone that I can be
And it just wouldn't feel right
If I didn't have you by my side, oh

You were there for me to love and care for me
When skies were gray
Whenever I was down, you were always there
To comfort me
And no one else can be what you have been to me
You will always be
You will always be the girl in my life
For all times

Mama, mama you know I love you
(I love you, ooh, you know I
love you)
Mama, mama you're the
queen of my heart
Your love is like tears
from the stars (Yes, it is)
Mama I just want you to
know
Lovin' you is like food to
my soul (Yes, it is, yes, it,
is, oh . . . oh . . . oh . . .)
(Yes, it is, yes, it is, yes it,
is, oh . . . oh . . . oh . . .)

Sister/Friend

by April Halprin Wayland

A sister provides comfort and understanding.

If I ever forget
how much you
feel
know
sense

may I remember
this April night
and you,
listening to my breaking voice
and blowing softly on my wet cheeks

POEM

by Langston Hughes

The following poem makes a statement about a lost friend.

I loved my friend.
He went away from me.
There's nothing more to say.
The poem ends,
Soft as it began—
I loved my friend.

Answering the BIG Question

When you do the following activities, consider the Big Question:
Who can we really count on?

WRITE TO LEARN In your Learner's Notebook, write a couple of sentences retelling the message or story of each poem. Then in one or two sentences, write what you've learned from these poems.

PARTNER TALK Work with a partner who has read these poems. Discuss the different people the speaker in each poem counted on. Then, if you feel comfortable, share a story with your partner about a time in your life when you counted on someone.

from THE

FELLOWSHIP
OF THE RING

by J. R. R. Tolkien

The Fellowship of the Ring is the first book in the *Lord of the Rings* trilogy. At this time, the hobbit Frodo Baggins and his companions are traveling to the place where the Ring of Power can be destroyed.

F rodo rose to his feet. A great weariness was on him, but his will was firm and his heart lighter. He spoke aloud to himself. 'I will do now what I must,' he said. 'This at least is plain: the evil of the Ring is already at work even in the Company, and the Ring must leave them before it does more harm. I will go alone. ❶ Some I cannot trust, and those I can trust are too dear to me: poor old Sam, and Merry and Pippin. Strider, too: his heart yearns for Minas Tirith, and he will be needed there, now Boromir has fallen into evil. I will go alone. At once.'

> **❶ Drawing Conclusions**
> Why did Frodo decide to "go alone"?

He went quickly down the path and came back to the lawn where Boromir had found him. Then he halted, listening. He thought he could hear cries and calls from the woods near the shore below.

'They'll be hunting for me,' he said. 'I wonder how long I have been away. Hours, I should think.' He hesitated. 'What can I do?' he muttered. 'I must go now or I shall never go. I shan't get a chance again. I hate leaving them, and like this without any explanation. But surely they will understand. Sam will. And what else can I do?'

Slowly he drew out the Ring and put it on once more. He vanished and passed down the hill, less than a rustle of the wind.

The others remained long by the river-side. For some time they had been silent, moving restlessly about it; but now they were sitting in a circle, and they were talking. Every now and again they made efforts to speak of other things, of their long road and many adventures; they questioned Aragorn concerning the <u>realm</u> of Gondor and its ancient history, and the <u>remnants</u> of its great works that could still be seen in this strange borderland of

Vo•cab•u•lary

realm (relm) land, kingdom
remnants (REM nentz) small parts remaining

the Emyn Muil: the stone kings and the seats of Lhaw and Hen, and the great Stair beside the falls of Rauros. But always their thoughts and words strayed back to Frodo and the Ring. What would Frodo choose to do? Why was he hesitating?

'He is debating which course is the most desperate, I think,' said Aragorn. 'And well he may. It is now more hopeless than ever for the Company to go east, since we have been tracked by Gollum, and must fear that the secret of our journey is already betrayed. But Minas Tirith is no nearer to the Fire and the destruction of the Burden.

'We may remain there for a while and make a brave stand; but the Lord Denethor and all his men cannot hope to do what even Elrond said was beyond his power: either to keep the Burden secret, or to hold off the full might of the Enemy when he comes to take it. Which way would any of us choose in Frodo's place? I do not know. Now indeed we miss Gandalf most.'

'Grievous is our loss,' said Legolas. 'Yet we must needs make up our minds without his aid. Why cannot we decide, and so help Frodo? Let us call him back and then vote! I should vote for Minas Tirith.' **2**

'And so should I,' said Gimli. 'We, of course, were only sent to help the <u>Bearer</u> along the road, to go no further than we wished; and none of us is under any oath or command to seek Mount Doom. Hard was my parting from Lothlorien. Yet I have come so far, and I say this: now we have reached the last choice, it is clear to me that I cannot leave Frodo. I would choose Minas Tirith, but if he does not, then I follow him.'

> **2 Drawing Conclusions**
> Why does Legolas think the group should take a vote?

'And I too will go with him,' said Legolas. 'It would be faithless now to say farewell.'

'It would indeed be a betrayal, if we all left him,' said Aragorn. 'But if he goes east, then all need not go with him; nor do I think

---

Vo·cab·u·lary

bearer (BAIR er) keeper; one in posession of

that all should. That <u>venture</u> is desperate: as much so for eight as for three or two, or one alone. If you would let me choose, then I should appoint three companions: Sam, who could not bear it otherwise; and Gimli; and myself. Boromir will return to his own city, where his father and his people need him; and with him the others should go, or at least Meriadoc and Peregrin, if Legolas is not willing to leave us.'

'That won't do at all!' cried Merry. 'We can't leave Frodo! Pippin and I always intended to go wherever he went, and we still do. But we did not realize what that would mean. It seemed different so far away, in the Shire or in Rivendell. It would be mad and cruel to let Frodo go to Mordor. Why can't we stop him?'

'We must stop him,' said Pippin. 'And that is what he is worrying about, I am sure. He knows we shan't agree to his going east. And he doesn't like to ask anyone to go with him, poor old fellow. Imagine it: going off to Mordor alone!' Pippin shuddered. 'But the dear silly old hobbit, he ought to know that he hasn't got to ask. He ought to know that if we can't stop him, we shan't leave him.'

'Begging your pardon,' said Sam. 'I don't think you understand my master at all. He isn't hesitating about which way to go. Of course not! What's the good of Minas Tirith anyway? To him, I mean, begging your pardon, Master Boromir,' he added, and turned. ❸ It was then that they discovered that Boromir, who at first had been sitting silent on the outside of the circle, was no longer there.

> **❸ Drawing Conclusions**
> Which character knows Frodo best?

'Now where's he got to?' cried Sam, looking worried. 'He's been a bit queer lately, to my mind. But anyway he's not in this business. He's off to his home, as he always said; and no blame to him. But Mr. Frodo, he knows

Vo•cab•u•lary

venture (VEN chur) a risky undertaking

he's got to find the Cracks of Doom, if he can. But he's afraid. Now it's come to the point, he's just plain terrified. That's what his trouble is. Of course he's had a bit of schooling, so to speak—we all have—since we left home, or he'd be so terrified he'd just fling the Ring in the River and bolt. But he's still too frightened to start. And he isn't worrying about us either: whether we'll go along with him or no. He knows we mean to. That's another thing that's bothering him. If he screws himself up to go, he'll want to go alone. Mark my words! We're going to have trouble when he comes back. For he'll screw himself up all right, as sure as his name's Baggins.'

'I believe you speak more wisely than any of us, Sam,' said Aragorn. 'And what shall we do, if you prove right?'

'Stop him! Don't let him go!' cried Pippin.

'I wonder?' said Aragorn. 'He is the Bearer, and the fate of the <u>Burden</u> is on him. I do not think that it is our part to drive him one way or the other. Nor do I think that we should succeed if we tried. There are other powers at work far stronger.'

'Well, I wish Frodo would "screw himself up" and come back, and let us get it over,' said Pippin. 'This waiting is horrible! Surely the time is up?'

'Yes,' said Aragorn. 'The hour is long passed. The morning is wearing away. We must call for him.' **4**

4 Drawing Conclusions
Why are some members of the company becoming impatient?

At that moment Boromir reappeared. He came out from the trees and walked towards them without speaking. His face looked grim and sad. He paused as if counting those that were present, and then sat down aloof, with his eyes on the ground.

'Where have you been, Boromir?' asked Aragorn. 'Have you seen Frodo?'

Vo•cab•u•lary
burden (BUR din) load

Boromir hesitated for a second. 'Yes, and no,' he answered slowly. 'Yes: I found him some way up the hill, and I spoke to him. I urged him to come to Minas Tirith and not to go east. I grew angry and he left me. He vanished. I have never seen such a thing happen before, though I have heard of it in tales. He must have put the Ring on. I could not find him again. I thought he would return to you.'

'Is that all that you have to say?' said Aragorn, looking hard and not too kindly at Boromir.

'Yes,' he answered. 'I will say no more yet.'

'This is bad!' cried Sam, jumping up. 'I don't know what this Man has been up to. Why should Mr. Frodo put the thing on? He didn't ought to have; and if he has, goodness knows what may have happened!'

'But he wouldn't keep it on,' said Merry. 'Not when he had escaped the unwelcome visitor, like Bilbo used to.'

'But where did he go? Where is he?' cried Pippin. 'He's been away ages now.'

'How long is it since you saw Frodo last, Boromir?' asked Aragorn.

'Half an hour, maybe,' he answered. 'Or it might be an hour. I have wandered for some time since. I do not know! I do not know!' He put his head in his hands, and sat as if bowed with grief.

'An hour since he vanished!' shouted Sam. 'We must try and find him at once. Come on!'

'Wait a moment!' cried Aragorn. 'We must divide up into pairs, and arrange—here, hold on! Wait!'

It was no good. They took no notice of him. Sam had dashed off first. Merry and Pippin had followed, and were already disappearing westward into the trees by the shore, shouting: Frodo! Frodo! in their clear, high, hobbit-voices. Legolas and Gimli were running. A sudden panic or madness seemed to have fallen on the Company.

'We shall all be scattered and lost,' groaned Aragorn. 'Boromir! I do not know what part you have played in this mischief, but help now! Go after those two young hobbits, and guard them at the least, even if you cannot find Frodo. Come back to this spot, if you find him, or any traces of him. I shall return soon.'

Aragorn sprang swiftly away and went in pursuit of Sam. Just as he reached the little lawn among the rowans he overtook him, toiling uphill, panting and calling, Frodo!

'Come with me, Sam!' he said. 'None of us should be alone. There is mischief about. I feel it. I am going to the top, to the Seat of Amon Hen, to see what may be seen. And look! It is as my heart guessed, Frodo went this way. Follow me, and keep your eyes open!' He sped up the path.

Sam did his best, but he could not keep up with Strider the Ranger, and soon fell behind. He had not gone far before Aragorn was out of sight ahead. Sam stopped and puffed. Suddenly he clapped his hand to his head.

'Whoa, Sam Gamgee!' he said aloud. 'Your legs are too short, so use your head! Let me see now! Boromir isn't lying, that's not his way; but he hasn't told us everything. Something scared Mr. Frodo badly. He screwed himself up to the point, sudden. He made up his mind at last—to go. Where to? Off east. Not without Sam? Yes, without even Sam. That's hard, cruel hard.'

Sam passed his hand over his eyes, brushing away the tears. 'Steady, Gamgee!' he said. 'Think, if you can! He can't fly across rivers, and he can't jump waterfalls. He's got no gear. So he's got to get back to the boats. Back to the boats! Back to the boats, Sam, like lightning!' **5**

Sam turned and bolted back down the path. He fell and cut his knees. Up he got and ran on. He came to the edge of the lawn of Parth Galen by the shore, where the boats were drawn up out of the water. No one was there. There seemed to be cries in the woods behind, but he did not heed them. He stood gazing for a moment, stock-still, gaping. A boat was sliding down the bank all by itself. With a shout Sam raced across the grass. The boat slipped into the water.

> **5 Determining Main Idea/ Supporting Details**
> How does Sam figure out where Frodo went?

'Coming, Mr. Frodo! Coming!' called Sam, and flung himself from the bank, clutching at the departing boat. He missed it by a yard. With a cry and a splash he fell face downward into deep swift water. Gurgling he went under, and the River closed over his curly head.

An exclamation of dismay came from the empty boat. A paddle swirled and the boat put about. Frodo was just in time to grasp Sam by the hair as he came up, bubbling and struggling. Fear was staring in his round brown eyes.

'Up you come, Sam my lad!' said Frodo. 'Now take my hand!'

'Save me, Mr. Frodo!' gasped Sam. 'I'm drownded. I can't see your hand.'

'Here it is. Don't pinch, lad! I won't let you go. Tread water and don't flounder, or you'll upset the boat. There now, get hold of the side, and let me use the paddle!'

With a few strokes Frodo brought the boat back to the bank, and Sam was able to scramble out, wet as a water-rat. Frodo took off the Ring and stepped ashore again.

'Of all the <u>confounded</u> <u>nuisances</u> you are the worst, Sam!' he said.

'Oh, Mr. Frodo, that's hard!' said Sam shivering. 'That's hard, trying to go without me and all. If I hadn't a guessed right, where would you be now?'

'Safely on my way.'

'Safely!' said Sam. 'All alone and without me to help you? I couldn't have a borne it, it'd have been the death of me.'

'It would be the death of you to come with me, Sam,' said Frodo, 'and I could not have borne that.'

'Not as certain as being left behind,' said Sam.

'But I am going to Mordor.'

'I know that well enough, Mr. Frodo. Of course you are. And I'm coming with you.'

'Now, Sam,' said Frodo, 'don't <u>hinder</u> me! The others will be coming back at any minute. If they catch me here, I shall have to argue and explain, and I shall never have the heart or the chance to get off. But I must go at once. It's the only way.'

'Of course it is,' answered Sam. 'But not alone. I'm coming too, or neither of us isn't going. I'll knock holes in all the boats first.' **6**

6 Responding
What is your opinion of Sam?

Frodo actually laughed. A sudden warmth and gladness touched his heart. 'Leave one!' he said. 'We'll need it. But you can't come like this without your gear or food or anything.'

'Just hold on a moment, and I'll get my stuff!' cried Sam eagerly. 'It's all ready. I thought we should be off today.' He rushed to the camping place, fished out his pack from the pile where Frodo had laid it when he emptied the boat of his

---

Vo•cab•u•lary

confounded (kawn FOWN did) confused
nuisances (NOO suns uz) annoying persons or things
hinder (HIN dur) to hold back, to get in the way

companions' goods, grabbed a spare blanket, and some extra packages of food, and ran back.

'So all my plan is spoilt!' said Frodo. 'It is no good trying to escape you. But I'm glad, Sam. I cannot tell you how glad. Come along! It is plain that we were meant to go together. We will go, and may the others find a safe road! Strider will look after them. I don't suppose we shall see them again.' **7**

'Yet we may, Mr. Frodo. We may,' said Sam.

So Frodo and Sam set off on the last stage of the Quest together. Frodo paddled away from the shore, and the River bore them swiftly away, down the western arm, and past the frowning cliffs of Tol Brandir. The roar of the great falls drew nearer. Even with such help as Sam could give, it was hard work to pass across the current at the southward end of the island and drive the boat eastward towards the far shore.

At length they came to land again upon the southern slopes of Amon Lhaw. There they found a shelving shore, and they drew the boat out, high above the water, and hid it as well as they could behind a great boulder. Then shouldering their burdens, they set off, seeking a path that would bring them over the grey hills of the Emyn Muil, and down into the Land of Shadow. ○

> **7 Synthesizing**
> What qualities does Frodo show?

Answering the BIG Question

When you do the following activities, consider the Big Question:
Who can we really count on?

WRITE TO LEARN Frodo and Sam both put each other's needs and safety ahead of their own. When was the last time you did something truly selfless? In your Learner's Notebook, write about a time when you put the needs of another before your own.

PARTNER TALK With a partner, discuss the qualities of someone you know you can count on.

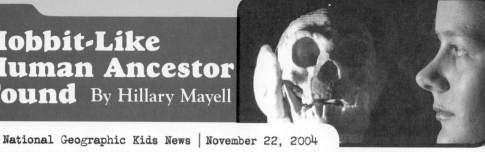

Hobbit-Like Human Ancestor Found By Hillary Mayell

National Geographic Kids News | November 22, 2004

Read about a startling discovery made on an island in Indonesia.

Scientists have found skeletons of a hobbit-like <u>species</u> of human that grew no larger than a three-year-old modern child. The tiny humans had skulls about the size of grapefruits and lived on a remote island in Indonesia 18,000 years ago.

The scientists discovered bones of the miniature humans in a cave on the island of Flores. Scientists named the new species *Homo floresiensis*, after the island.

But dig workers called them hobbits after the tiny creatures from the *Lord of the Rings* books. **1**

One female skeleton stood just 3.3 feet (1 meter) tall, weighed about 55 pounds (25 kilograms), and was around 30 years old at the time of her death.

> **1 Responding**
> Why is this discovery important?

"They [the hobbit-like species] had slightly longer arms than us. . . . they had hard, thicker eyebrow ridges than us, a sharply sloping forehead, and no chin," scientist Richard Roberts said.

"While they don't look like modern humans, some of their behaviors were surprisingly human," scientist Peter Brown said.

The "hobbits" used fire in <u>hearths</u> for cooking and hunted stegodon, a primitive dwarf elephant found on the island.

The hobbit-like creatures lived on Flores as recently as 13,000 years ago, which means they would have lived at the same time as modern

Vo•cab•u•lary

species (SPEE sheez) a category of living organisms consisting of similar individuals capable of interbreeding
hearths (harths) fireplace floors

humans, scientists say.

But it is unknown whether the creatures lived alongside modern humans. ❷

Still, rumors, myths, and legends of tiny creatures have swirled around the isolated island for centuries. It's certainly possible that they interacted with modern humans, according to the researchers.

Researchers are also anxious to study how and why the creatures came to be so small.

There is no record of human adults ever being that small. Modern Pygmies from Africa are considerably taller at about 4.6 to nearly 5 feet (1.4 to 1.5 meters) tall.

"I could not have predicted such a discovery in a million years," said Chris Stringer of the Natural History Museum in London. "This find shows us how much we still have to learn. . . ."

The study was published in the October 28, 2004, issue of *Nature*. ○

Answering the BIG Question

When you do the following activities, consider the Big Question:
Who can we really count on?

WRITE TO LEARN In some ways these tiny creatures are similar to modern humans, and in other ways they differ. Write a brief entry in your Learner's Notebook describing the main similarities and differences.

LITERATURE GROUPS Scientists were amazed to discover the skeletons of hobbit-like creatures in Indonesia. Join a couple of students who have read this selection. Discuss one or two other recent scientific discoveries that may have surprised you.

Vo•cab•u•lary

interacted (in tur AK ted) acted with others

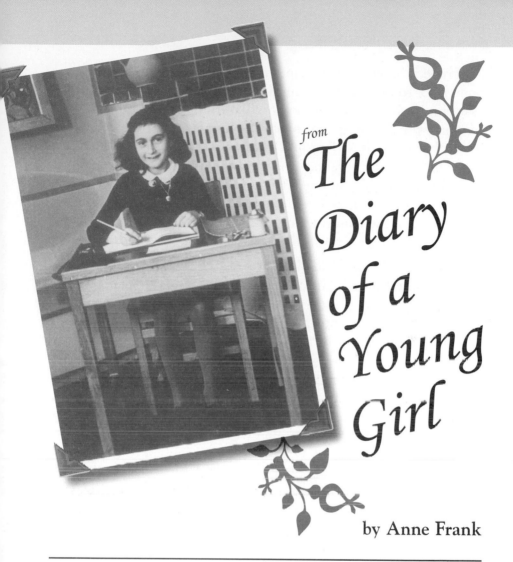

from

The Diary of a Young Girl

by Anne Frank

Anne Frank creates an unusual close friend in order to share her deepest feelings.

I haven't written for a few days, because I wanted first of all to think about my diary. It's an odd idea for someone like me to keep a diary; not only because I have never done so before, but because it seems to me that neither I—nor for that matter anyone else—will be interested in the unbosomings of a thirteen-year-old schoolgirl. Still, what does that matter? I want to write, but more than that, I want to bring out all kinds of things that lie buried deep in my heart.

There is a saying that "paper is more patient than man"; it came back to me on one of my slightly <u>melancholy</u> days, while I sat chin in hand, feeling too bored and limp even to make up my mind whether to go out or stay at home. Yes, there is no doubt that paper is patient and as I don't intend to show this cardboard-covered notebook, bearing the proud name of "diary," to anyone, unless I find a real friend, boy or girl, probably nobody cares. And now I come to the root of the matter, the reason for my starting a diary: it is that I have no such real friend. ❶

> ❶ **Determining Main Idea**
> What is the main point Anne is making in this paragraph?

Let me put it more clearly, since no one will believe that a girl of thirteen feels herself quite alone in the world, nor is it so. I have darling parents and a sister of sixteen. I know about thirty people whom one might call friends—I have strings of boy friends, anxious to catch a glimpse of me and who, failing that, peep at me through mirrors in class. I have relations, aunts and uncles, who are darlings too, a good home, no—I don't seem to lack anything. But it's the same with all my friends, just fun and joking, nothing more. I can never bring myself to talk of anything outside the common round. We don't seem to be able to get any closer, that is the root of the trouble. Perhaps I lack confidence, but anyway, there it is, a stubborn fact, and I don't seem to be able to do anything about it.

Hence, this diary. In order to enhance in my mind's eye the picture of the friend for whom I have waited so long, I don't want to set down a series of bald facts in a diary like most people do, but I want this diary itself to be my friend, and I shall call my friend Kitty. No one will grasp what I'm talking about if I begin my letters to Kitty just out of the blue, so albeit unwillingly, I will start by sketching in brief the story of my life.

My father was thirty-six when he married my mother, who was then twenty-five. My sister Margot was born in 1926 in

Vo•cab•u•lary

melancholy (MEL en kawl ee) sad

Frankfort-on-Main, I followed on June 12, 1929, and, as we are Jewish, we <u>emigrated</u> to Holland in 1933, where my father was appointed Managing Director of Travies N.V. This firm is in close relationship with the firm of Kolen & Co. in the same building, of which my father is a partner.

The rest of the family, however, felt the full impact of Hitler's anti-Jewish laws, so life was filled with anxiety. In 1938 after the <u>pogroms</u>, my two uncles (my mother's brothers) escaped to the U.S.A. My old grandmother came to us, she was then seventy-three. After May 1940 good times rapidly fled: first the war, then the <u>capitulation</u>, followed by the arrival of the Germans, which is when the sufferings of us Jews really began. Anti-Jewish decrees followed each other in quick succession. Jews must wear a yellow star, Jews must hand in their bicycles, Jews are banned from trains and are forbidden to drive. Jews are only allowed to do their shopping between three and five o'clock and then in shops which bear the placard "Jewish shop." Jews must be indoors by eight o'clock and cannot even sit in their own gardens after that hour. Jews are forbidden to visit theaters, cinemas, and other places of entertainment. Jews may not take part in public sports. Swimming baths, tennis courts, hockey fields, and other sports grounds are all prohibited to them.

Vo•cab•u•lary

emigrated (EM ih grayt ud) moved or migrated out of one country or region to another
pogroms (POH grumz) organized massacres of helpless people
capitulation (kuh pih chuh LAY shun) surrender

Jews may not visit Christians. Jews must go to Jewish schools, and many more restrictions of a similar kind. ❷

So we could not do this and were forbidden to do that. But life went on in spite of it all. Jopie used to say to me, "You're scared to do anything, because it may be forbidden." Our freedom was strictly limited. Yet things were still bearable.

❷ **Synthesizing**
How did Hitler's treatment of the Jews affect Anne?

Granny died in January 1942; no one will ever know how much she is present in my thoughts and how much I love her still.

In 1934 I went to school at the Montessori Kindergarten and continued there. It was at the end of the school year, I was in form 6B, when I had to say good-by to Mrs. K. We both wept, it was very sad. In 1941 I went, with my sister Margot, to the Jewish Secondary School, she into the fourth form and I into the first.

So far everything is all right with the four of us and here I come to the present day. ○

Answering the BIG Question

When you do the following activities, consider the Big Question:
Who can we really count on?

WRITE TO LEARN Think about a time when you wanted to confide in a friend but found it difficult. What did you want to say? Why was it difficult? Make an entry explaining the situation in your Learner's Notebook.

PARTNER TALK With another student who has read this selection, discuss the restrictions placed on Jews during the Nazi occupation of Holland. Discuss whether it is possible for something like this to happen again.

Baby Hippo Orphan Finds a Friend

By Catherine Clarke Fox

Find out what happens to a baby hippo when it no longer has its mother to count on.

Have you noticed that sometimes the most unlikely pairs form the best friendships? Late last December, flood waters in the East African country of Kenya swept a herd of hippopotamuses down the Sabaki River and into the Indian Ocean. After a few days, most of them struggled to shore and returned inland.

Then, right after the Asian <u>tsunami</u> hit on December 26, local people spotted a baby hippo in the rough surf, apparently left behind by the herd. They were worried.

Hippos live around fresh water, and the people figured the salt water wasn't good for the little fellow. Besides, he had no mother to look out for him.

After hours of effort, they caught the big baby (about 600 pounds, or 270 kilograms). They named him Owen after one of his rescuers. ❶

> ❶ **Determining Main Idea/ Supporting Details**
> What is the main idea of this section? What details help explain the main idea?

Vo·cab·u·lary

tsunami (soo NAH mee) an enormous, potentially destructive wave caused by an earthquake or a volcano erupting on the bottom of the ocean

Wildlife officials took Owen the hippo to the safety of Haller Park, a <u>sanctuary</u> for wild animals in the port city of Mombasa. To their surprise, Owen, about a year old, trotted right up to a giant gray tortoise.

Tortoises are among the longest-living creatures on Earth. This one's name is Mzee, which means "old man" in the Swahili language. He is more than a hundred years old.

"Mzee hissed, lifted himself up off the ground, and tried to run," reported Paula Kahumbu, an ecologist in charge of Haller Park. (Ecologists study how living things relate to their surroundings.) "But by the next morning, they were together!"

They have been together ever since, even staying close and touching when they sleep.

Owen could weigh more than 6,000 pounds (2,700 kilograms) when he is grown— heavier than a minivan. Eventually he will be introduced to Cleo, an adult hippo, so he can be with his own kind.

But Kahumbu said Owen and Mzee will still spend time together if they wish. ❷ ○

> ❷ **Synthesizing**
> What makes friendships like this one so appealing?

Answering the BIG Question

When you do the following activities, consider the Big Question:
Who can we really count on?

WRITE TO LEARN Think about the unlikely friendship in this article. Then write a brief entry in your Learner's Notebook about an unlikely friendship you have observed.

PARTNER TALK Work with a partner to discuss what hardships people might experience during a natural disaster. Then focus on one hardship; discuss some possible ways that people might help each other through a difficult time.

Vo•cab•u•lary

sanctuary (SANK choo air ee) a safe place for birds and wild animals

When the Rattlesnake Sounds

by Alice Childress

Harriet Tubman helped more than 300 slaves reach freedom on the Underground Railroad. The "stations" on this railroad were houses where escaping slaves could hide.

Underground Railroad Key:

← Approximated
flight routes

■ Free states

■ Slave states

■ Territories

Characters

Harriet Tubman. An experienced leader who knows how to handle people with firmness . . . and love.

Lennie. A strong, determined, no-nonsense kind of young woman.

Celia. A young woman who has the tendency to get fed up when the going is grubby and ordinary.

Setting

Time. Very close to the end of legal slavery.

Place. Cape May, New Jersey.

Scene

A hotel laundry room. Harriet, Lennie, and Celia are washing clothes. Harriet and Lennie work <u>vigorously</u>, absorbed in the task. Celia is slowing up and finally stops.

Celia. (*cautiously watching* Harriet *and* Lennie) Lord, I'm tired. (*others keep working*) Seem like we workin way past our dinnertime, don't it? Harriet? Lennie?

Lennie. Not much past dinner. It feels like about one o'clock.

Harriet. We're gonna stop and eat by 'n by. We'll put out five

---

Vo·cab·u·lary

vigorously (VIG ur us lee) in a way that shows physical strength

bundles of wash today. Yesterday was only four.

Celia. Only four? When I went to bed last night, I cried, I was so bone-weary. Only? How can four bundles of wash be only?

Harriet. Just a while longer, Celia. Let's sing. When you singin, the work goes fast. You pick a song, Lennie.

Lennie. (*decides to pick one that will annoy* Celia) Wadin in the water, wadin in the water (*children*). Wadin in the water, God gonna trouble the water. (Harriet *joins her in singing.*)

Celia. (*drying her hands on her apron*) I want my dinner now. I'm hungry.

Lennie. We all hungry, Celia. Can't you hold out a little more?

Celia. If we all hungry, why don't we all eat? We been up since seven this mornin . . . workin. For what? Why?

Lennie. You know why! We got to finish five bundles.

Celia. (*to the heavens above*) Five bundles for what?

Lennie. For a dollar and a quarter, that's what! (*grumbling*) I'm tellin you . . . some people.

Harriet. (*Sensing trouble, she stops washing.*) Celia is right, Lennie. It's not good to kill yourself workin.

Lennie. (*her eyes on* Celia) Did you fix it again, Harriet? We suppose to take turns. I take a turn, you take a turn, then . . .

Harriet. (*hastily cutting her off*) I got some nice corn bread and some side meat. The coffee should be ready. (*handing out paper parcels to the girls*) We need to rest awhile. Here, Celia, and that's yours Lennie. (*going back to her tub*) I'll just wash out these few more pieces before my water turns cold. ❶

Lennie. I ain't restin unless you rest too. Not like some people I know.

Celia. She keep sayin some people.

> ❶ **Drawing Conclusions** Why does Harriet say they should rest?

Vo•cab•u•lary

parcels (PAHR selz) packages

Wonder who she means?

Harriet. (*with a sigh*) I'll stop too.

Celia. (*looking at the pile of unwashed clothes as she unwraps her lunch*) White folks love white clothes and they love to sit in the grass too . . . and I'm sick of scrubbin grass stains.

Harriet. Well, we need the money.

Celia. (*puts down her lunch and snatches up a <u>flouncy</u> white dress*) Look at all the money they got. This cost every bit of twelve dollars. (*imitating the hotel guests*) Spendin the summer in a big hotel, ridin round in carriages. (*drops her airy act and goes back to anger*) If just one of em give us what she spend in a week . . . we wouldn't have to work two months in no hotel laundry.

Lennie. I got a life-size picture of them givin you that much money. They ain't gonna give you nothin, so you better be glad you got the chance to earn some.

Celia. Scrubbin! Ain't that a damn somethin to be glad about? Excuse me Harriet, I meant to say dern or drat.

Harriet. Celia got somethin on her mind, and she need to talk, so let her talk, Lennie. But no dammin, dernin, or drattin either. All here got more manners than to cuss.

Lennie. (*as she looks at* Harriet's *food*) Is that your dinner? You ain't got no meat on your bread, Harriet.

Harriet. I don't too much like meat.

Lennie. I know who do. Some people.

Celia. (*bursting out at* Harriet) Stop sayin that! You do too like meat! Stop makin out like you don't. You goin without so you can save another nickel. ❷ Yall drivin me outta my head. Maybe I'm just not suited for this kind of thing.

> ❷ **Responding**
> What do you think of Celia?

Vo•cab•u•lary

flouncy (FLOWN see) like decorative material that is gathered or pleated; frilly

Lennie. But I am, huh?

Harriet. (*quietly and seriously*) You tired of this bargain we made? You sorry about it and don't know how to quit?

Lennie. (*flaring with anger*) She promised and she got to stick by it! Your father is a <u>deacon</u> of the church . . . and if you don't keep your word, you gonna bring disgrace down on him and every member of your family.

Harriet. Lennie, don't be so brash. Mother and father is one thing . . . child is another. Each one stands upon his own deeds. She don't have to stay. Celia, you can go if you want.

Celia. I don't really want to get out of it. But I want some of my money for myself. I'm tired of sleepin three in a room. I want to spend a little of the money . . . just a little, Harriet. Buy a few treats.

Lennie. She's jealous of them rich white ladies . . . cause they got silk <u>parasols</u> to match they dresses. I heard her say it. "Wish I had me a silk parasol."

Harriet. We eatin and sleepin. We spend for that and nothin more . . . that was the bargain.

Celia. (*to Lennie*) I could own a silk parasol and carry it . . . without actin like a field hand.

Harriet. I been a field hand, children. Harness to a plow like a workhorse.

Celia. Scuse me, I'm sorry.

Lennie. (*really sarcastic*) Celia, that don't sound nothin like them big speeches you used to make in church meetin. (*mocking Celia*) "I'll die for my freedom!" . . . Had everybody whoopin and hollerin every time you open your mouth, whole church stompin and shoutin amen.

Vo·cab·u·lary

deacon (DEE kun) a church officer who is not an ordained minister
parasols (PAR eh sawlz) light umbrellas used for protection from the sun

Celia. (*sadly*) I remember how it was. (*The women remove their aprons and Harriet takes her place center stage. Church music in from off-stage or recording of "The Old Ship of Zion," or any of the A.M.E. Zion songs. Harriet Tubman was a member of that church. She addresses the audience as though they are the* <u>congregation</u>.)

Harriet. (*Music and humming are in low as she speaks.*) God bless you, brothers and sisters, bless you, children.

Offstage Voices plus Lennie and Celia. Amen . . . Amen . . . Bless God.

Harriet. I thank the good Lord for the support of the African Methodist Episcopal Zion Church in the freedom struggle. There is comfort and good fellowship here.

Church Voices. Yes, Lord. Amen.

Harriet. Not like hidin in the bitter cold, with the huntin dogs followin you down with no restin place in sight.

We had to give the little babies <u>paregoric</u> so they wouldn't cry and let the paddy-rollers know where to find us. We crossed some lonely roads and rivers . . . the dark of the night around us, the clouds cuttin off the sight of the North Star. But everything was all right cause where I go . . . God goes . . . and I carry a gun . . . two guns . . . a hand pistol and a shoulder rifle . . . just in case the Lord tell me I got to use it!

Church Voices. Amen! Speak! Praise the holy name! Amen!

Harriet. I thank the Father for the help and assistance of the Society of Friends and the <u>abolitionists</u>, and all well-wishers.

Vo•cab•u•lary

congregation (kawn greh GAY shun) a gathering of people for worship
paregoric (pair eh GOR ik) medicine that causes drowsiness in most people
abolitionists (ab uh LI shun ists) people who favor abolishing, or getting rid of, a particular law or custom; specifically those who favored abolishing slavery

Church Voices. Amen, Amen, Amen.

Harriet. But as I put my hand to the plow to do the work of
Freedom, so I also put my money into the work. I have none
now, so I will spend my summer washin and ironin so that
when the fall come I have some of my own to put . . . to buy
food, medicine, paregoric for the babies, and ammunition for
the pistol . . . Lord grant I never use it. Any ladies here want

People dug tunnels to hide slaves until they could be moved to freedom.

to go with me to wash clothes and give the money to free our slave brethren?

Lennie. *(stands by Harriet's side)* If you would have me, Mrs. Tubman, it would be the greatest honor, a great honor indeed.

Harriet. Thank you, my daughter.

Celia. *(stands up and throws her arms out in a Joan of Arc gesture)* I'll die for my freedom! Take me, Sister! I'm ready to fight the good fight. Hallelujah!

Church Voices. *(Celia has set the church to rocking.)* Glory! Glory! Hallelujah! Fight the good fight! Amen! *(Music fades out as women don their aprons again.)*

Celia. I remember how it was, Lennie, and the promise I made. But how much can we get like this? Maybe if everybody worked and gave their money to the Underground, it would mean somethin. This way I just can't see it, but I believe in freedom and I understand.

Harriet. Ain't no such thing as only "understandin." Understandin mean action. ❸ You have to look after what Celia does . . . and if nobody else do nothin, you got to. Freedom is just a baby, and you its mother. You don't stop lovin and carin for it just cause others don't care.

> ❸ **Determining Main Idea/ Supporting Details**
> What does Harriet mean when she says, "understandin mean action"?

Celia. Maybe it's easy to talk like that when you Moses. It's easy to kill yourself for somethin when thousands of people be cheerin you on. Lennie and Celia don't mean nothin to nobody. We could die here and nobody would know or care.

Lennie. Don't you talk for me! Ain't nothin greater to me than to be able to say . . . "I, Lennie Brown, scrubbed clothes side by side with Moses." If you lookin for praise, you don't belong here.

Harriet. Children, let us keep peace. We act like we hate each other worse than we hate the slaveowner.

Celia. I know what I sound like . . . *(falls at Harriet's feet and holds out her hands)* Oh, Harriet, my hands are skinned sore.

Lennie. Do, Jesus, look at Celia's hands.

Harriet. *(turns Celia's head and searches for the truth)* But it ain't your hands that's really botherin you. It ain't food, it ain't sleepin three in a room, and it ain't about silk parasols. What's botherin you, Celia?

Celia. I'm so shame for feelin the way I do. Lord knows I'm shame.

Harriet. Tell it. Speak your shame.

Celia. I'm scared. If these people in this hotel knew who you was. Forty thousand dollars' reward out for you! ❹

❹ **Determining Main Idea/ Supporting Details** What scares Celia most?

Lennie. *(dashes to the door to see if anyone is around to listen)* Hush your fool mouth! Moses got the charm. Slave holder will never catch Moses.

Celia. I'm so shame. All those other things just lies. I ain't so terrible tired. I'm just scared and shame cause I'm afraid. Me talkin so big. Sure, I'd work all summer and give the money to the Underground. It did sound so good in the meetin where it was all warm and friendly. Now I'm scared of gettin into trouble. I never been no slave. And I'm scared of nothin round me but white folks.

Lennie. We ain't got no room for no rabbity, <u>timid</u> kinda women in this work.

Harriet. Oh, yes, Lennie, we got room for the timid and the brave. Poor little Celia. Child, you lookin at a woman who's been plenty afraid. When the rattlesnake sounds a warnin . . . it's time to be scared. Ain't that natural? When I run away was nobody to cheer me on . . . don't you think I was scared?

Vo•cab•u•lary

timid (TIM id) fearful

Lennie. But you got to freedom.

Harriet. (*The feeling of a "meeting" begins.*) Oh, but when I found I'd crossed that line! There was such a glory over everything. The sun came shinin like gold through the trees.

Lennie. (*feels like she is at church meeting*) You felt like you was in heaven! You was free!

Harriet. But there was no one to welcome me in the land of freedom. I was a stranger in a strange land. My home, after all, was down in the old cabin quarters with the ones I knew and loved . . . my slave mother and father, brothers, sisters, and friends. Aunt Day . . . she used to be <u>midwife</u>, tend the sick, bury the dead. Two field hands I knew, they used to ease some of the work off the women who was expectin. There I was standin on free land, with my heart back down there with them. What good is freedom without your people?

Lennie. Go on, Harriet!

Harriet. And so to this solemn <u>resolution</u> I come: As I was free . . . they would be free also.

Lennie. Praise God, that's Harriet Tubman!

Harriet. Sometimes I was scared in the icy river. Chilled to the bone and just might drown.

Lennie. But you got cross.

Harriet. I was scared in the dark and the swamp . . . but I came to the light. Most times I was full of hatred for the white folks.

Lennie. And you came to the Friends.

Harriet. And I came to John Brown. (*offstage music . . . soft violin . . . sound of voices ad-libbing at a reception*) There was this big, fine affair. A reception. Abolitionist reception. The ladies were all dressed in lovely gowns, made by free labor.

Vo•cab•u•lary

midwife (MID wyf) a person, usually a woman, trained to assist women in childbirth

resolution (rez uh LOO shun) a firm decision to take a certain course of action

I was in my best too . . . but that wasn't too much better than what I'm standin in. They had pretty cakes and a punch bowl . . . the grandest party. Violin music . . . what you call elegant. There was a goodly crowd, and I was way on the other side of the room, away from the main door where the people would enter. Everybody called him Captain Brown . . . Captain. (Harriet *moves to the far side of the stage and turns toward the opposite door to illustrate the distance between her and Captain Brown.*)

Captain John Brown

Harriet. The whisper started way down the hall and came through the room . . . "It's Captain Brown. He's here. Captain Brown is about to enter." Then he came in the door. He was a fine, stern-lookin gentleman . . . goodness glowed from his face like a burnin light. The room got quiet. He looked all around until he saw me. Mind now, we had never met. The ladies and gentlemen were all tryin to meet him . . . Oh, it was Captain, Captain, Captain. He held up his hand. There was silence, then he said . . . "The first I see is General Tubman. The second is General Tubman. The third is General Tubman." He crossed the room and bowed to me . . . and I shook his hand.

Lennie. And he died for us, didn't he?

Harriet. Celia, he was a brave man, but I believe he must have been scared sometimes. But he did what he had to do.

Celia. I guess he was just brave. Some folks braver than others.

Harriet. I was with hundreds of brave black men on battleground. I was there, Celia. We saw the lightning and that was the guns, then we heard the thunder and that was the big guns, then we heard the rain falling . . . and that was the drops of blood. And when we came to get the crops, it was dead men we reaped.

Lennie. Fightin for us to be free. I guess they musta been scared sometimes.

Harriet. Give me your hand, Celia. Look, see the skin broken across the knuckles. Counta you some man or woman gonna have warm socks and boots to help em get to freedom. See the cuts the lye soap put in your skin. Counta you some little baby is gonna be born on free soil. It won't matter to him that you was afraid, won't matter that he did not know your name. Won't nothin count ceptin he's free. A livin monument to Celia's work. (*Celia cries.*) You go to the room and rest. Maybe you might want to stay here after you think about it.

Lennie. Sure, Celia . . . think bout it. We can manage. And if you want to go home, we won't hold it against you. I ought not to have said what I did. Sometimes I get scared myself . . . but it

Allen Chapel African Methodist Episcopal (A.M.E.) Church

makes me act evil and brave, you know? **5**

5 Synthesizing
How has Lennie changed?

Celia. I don't want to go home. Guess there's worse things than fear. I'm glad to know I don't have to be shame about it.

Harriet. That's right. If you was home doin nothin, what would you have to be fraid bout? That's when a woman oughta feel shame, shame to her very soul.

Celia. (*Gathers up clothes, places them in tub, starts working. Harriet goes to her tub.*) If we sing, the work goes faster.

Lennie. (*goes to her tub*) Your time to pick a song, Celia.

Celia. (*Celia starts scrubbing. They all work for a few moments. Celia has decided on a song. She sings out.*)

Oh, Lord, I don't feel no ways tired
Children, Oh, Glory Hallelujah
For I hope to shout Glory when this world is all on fire
Oh, Glory, Hallelujah
(*The others join her on the second round.*)
Oh, Lord, I don't feel no ways tired . . .

CURTAIN ○

Answering the BIG Question

When you do the following activities, consider the Big Question:
Who can we really count on?

WRITE TO LEARN Celia once claimed that she would die for her freedom. Later, she expresses fear and complains about the physical demands of her work. Think about a time when you made a difficult commitment and people were counting on you. Write about your experience in your Learner's Notebook.

LITERATURE GROUPS Get together with two or three other students who have read this selection. Discuss a struggle against injustice that you see in the world today. What are some people doing to change the situation?

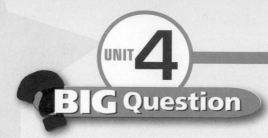

Who influences us and how do they do so?

Why do we make the choices we do? Sometimes our friends or what we see on TV pressures us. Other times we strive to be like the people we admire. The selections in this unit will ask you to think about the question: **Who influences us and how do they do so?**

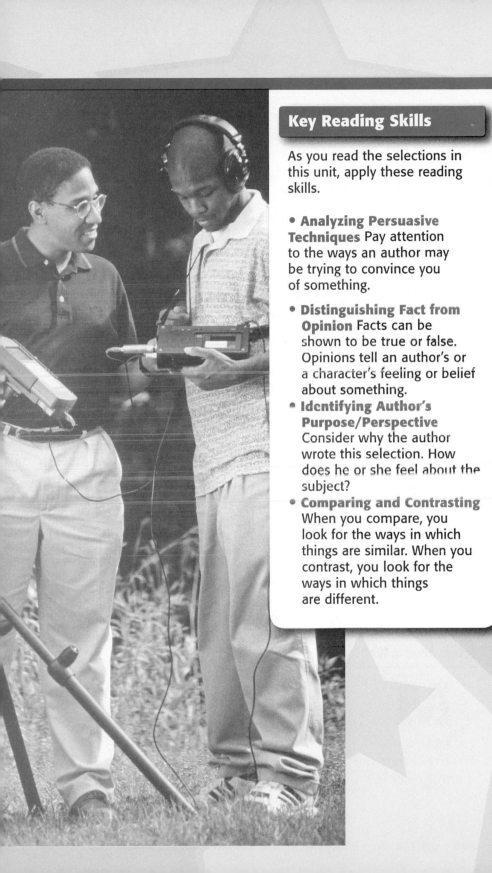

Key Reading Skills

As you read the selections in this unit, apply these reading skills.

• **Analyzing Persuasive Techniques** Pay attention to the ways an author may be trying to convince you of something.

• **Distinguishing Fact from Opinion** Facts can be shown to be true or false. Opinions tell an author's or a character's feeling or belief about something.

• **Identifying Author's Purpose/Perspective** Consider why the author wrote this selection. How does he or she feel about the subject?

• **Comparing and Contrasting** When you compare, you look for the ways in which things are similar. When you contrast, you look for the ways in which things are different.

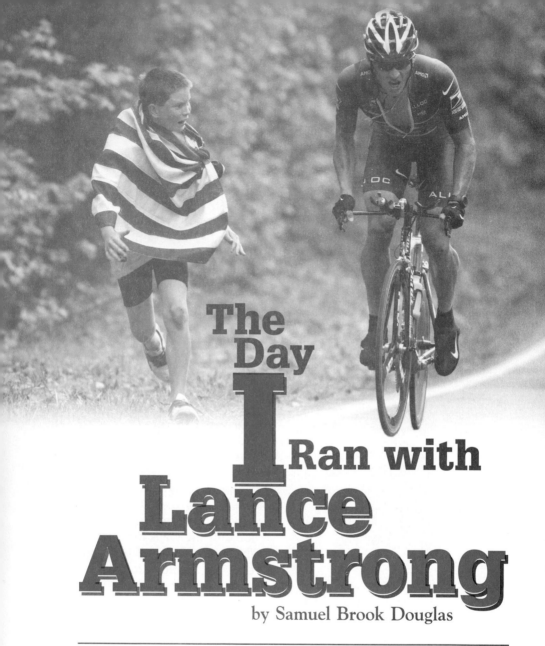

The Day I Ran with Lance Armstrong

by Samuel Brook Douglas

How does it feel to meet your hero?

My journey with cycling started very early. When I was two years old, I rode my first two miles on a bike. When I was five, I rode my first ten miles and learned how to ride without training wheels.

I wanted a real cycling outfit so badly that I chose to be Lance Armstrong for Halloween when I was eight years old.

I loved cycling so much that I even had a Tour de France birthday party. My friends and I biked all around the Berry College campus. My mom added flag stickers to our helmets when we pretended to be riding in European countries.

When I was nine, my dad, Uncle Dean, and I rode on bicycles on part of the Bike Ride Across Georgia.

When I was in fourth grade, I wrote this poem:

Samuel
Smart, handsome
I'm as fast as a cheetah
Love of Lance Armstrong and God
Who feels fearless
Who needs parents
Who would like to see the next Tour de France
Part of a big family Douglas **1**

When my parents read my poem, they decided we should all see the next Tour de France. They kept our trip a secret and told me only two weeks before leaving for Europe. I was very excited.

> **1 Identifying Author's Perspective**
> How does Samuel feel about Lance Armstrong?

We hiked three miles up the rocky Pyrenees Mountains to get our first glimpse of the Tour de France. We were very excited when the cyclists rode swiftly up the steep mountain.

We then followed the tour to Sabres, a small village. My brothers and I saw helicopters land, bringing officials to view the race. My brothers and I were yelling loudly at the cyclists: "Lance, Lance, Lance." Lance looked up at us to see if he recognized us and smiled. We enjoyed seeing many beautiful sights, especially the fields of sunflowers.

During the time trials in Nantes, we waited six long hours in the pouring rain to see Lance again.

We went to Paris to watch the final stage of the 2003 Tour

de France. The cyclists raced through the cobblestone streets of Champs-Elysees.

I thought that this was the end of my dream. Then in February 2004, it was announced that Lance Armstrong would be participating in the 2004 Tour de Georgia. My whole family starting chanting, "We went to France to see Lance, and now he is following us home to Rome!"

Stage three of the 2004 Tour de Georgia took the cyclists up the very steep Clock Tower Hill in downtown Rome, Georgia.

Lance won stage three, but not the Yellow Jersey.

Stage four of the Tour de Georgia was a steep climb up Mt. Alto. This was a time trial race where racers go one-by-one against the clock. We positioned ourselves on a steep incline to get a good view of each rider.

It was then that I decided to wear the American flag as a cape and run beside each and every rider to encourage him up the mountain.

As Lance cycled up the mountain, I cheered, "Lance, I saw you in France," and he answered, "Thanks!" I had spoken to my hero. I thought this was the end of my dream.

The next morning the whole world would see Lance and me on the front page of their newspapers. I thought this was the end of my dream. ❷

I was determined to get Lance Armstrong's autograph on our photo. I waited outside his team bus. Soon, a man emerged from the bus and said, "Aren't you the kid in the newspaper with Lance?"

❷ **Comparing and Contrasting**
How was Samuel's experience in Georgia like or different from the one in France?

I was allowed to walk beyond the barrier with a VIP pass and was given VIP treatment. I was presented with a U.S. Postal hat.

After the conclusion of stage seven of the Tour de Georgia, Lance Armstrong returned to his team bus. It was then that he autographed the newspaper with our photo inside and gave me his

water bottle. I thought this was the end of my dream.

Four days later, I learned the photo of Lance Armstrong and me would be featured in the May 2004 edition of *Sports Illustrated*.

Is this truly the end of my story, or is there more to be written? Only time will tell! Maybe one day, I will be a cyclist in a race and a little boy will be encouraging me up a steep hill. **3** ○

—*Samuel Brook Douglas, 11, Georgia*

3 Identifying Author's Purpose
Why did Samuel write the article?

Answering the BIG Question

When you do the following activities, consider the Big Question:
Who influences us and how do they do so?

WRITE TO LEARN Samuel ran up the hill to encourage the riders going up the steep hill in the Tour de Georgia. How did Lance Armstrong encourage Samuel? How do you think this event influenced his life? Write your answers in your Learner's Notebook.

PARTNER TALK Whom do you admire most? Why? Discuss your answers with a classmate.

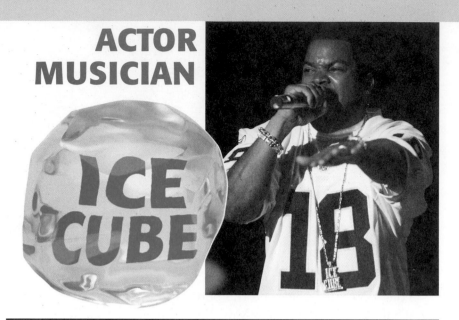

ACTOR
MUSICIAN

He's a rapper, writer, actor, and major celebrity. But whom does Ice Cube look up to?

by McClain J., Kansas City, MO,
and Angela R., Gibson, AZ

"**A**re We There Yet?" is his latest movie, but it's a <u>rhetorical</u> question because the man known as Ice Cube is most definitely there— at the top. **1**

Ice Cube is an appropriate nickname for a man as multifaceted as O'Shea Jackson. From shaping gangster rap in the '90s to writing and starring in movies, this 35-year-old native of South Central Los Angeles has become a force in Hollywood. Whether you have his CDs or plan to see his latest movie, Ice Cube demands attention.

1 Identifying Author's Perspective
What does the author think about Ice Cube?

Vo•cab•u•lary

rhetorical (ruh TOR ik uhl) a question asked for effect, not for a reply

Famous for his words and opinions, Ice Cube had this to say about writing in our pre-interview chat:

Teen Ink sounds like a great thing because people really underestimate the voice of kids, of youngsters. That's one of the reasons we got into hip-hop music: to be able to have some kind of voice, to be able to state our opinions to whomever would listen. And you have a magazine just dedicated to that, which is very smart. You know, it'd be smart if adults picked it up and actually read it. They'd learn a lot about themselves and their kids.

You know, everything starts with the writing—I don't care if you are doing a song or a movie or an article, instructions—everything starts with writing.

I have four kids, a son who just turned 18, a 13-year-old son, a 10-year-old daughter, and a four-year-old son. A lot of parents forget how it was to be their children's ages. Never forget how it was to be their age—that is the key, and remember what you went through. Remember what you thought of the world and don't forget, don't get caught up in your own age.

Angela: I'd like to know whom you admired most growing up and who had the greatest influence on you?

I was fortunate to have my father and brother with me. My brother is nine years older than myself. I looked up to both of them because they were always available, always there with anything I needed to help me get through the day, you know, living in South Central Los Angeles and trying not to get caught in all the traps it had. So I have to say my father and my brother had the biggest influence on me.

You know, I love people like entertainers and athletes but, my pops always told me, those famous people don't put no food on your table. ❷

Keep everything in perspective. You know, they get paid for what they are doing, you kind of give up your emotions for free so, you know, that always put

❷ **Comparing and Contrasting** How does Ice Cube compare celebrities' impact on him with the influence of his father and brother?

everything in perspective about who is really having an influence on my life.

McClain: What is the biggest obstacle you've had to face?

That's hard to sum up, but it's kind of always trying to show people that you can do it.

A lot of people love to doubt everybody but themselves, or you have to come in with <u>accolades</u> before they respect what you can do. So, growing up being in the business is always "give me a chance to show you I can do what I say I can do." That's been the biggest obstacle.

A: Do you think music (or any creative works for that matter) should be censored?

No, I think censorship is dangerous. Because it pulls out questions—who are the censors? What do they know? You know what I mean, that's really what it boils down to.

I think all art should have age limits, you know? There is nothing wrong with putting age limits on things. Categories, a rating system for movies—there is nothing wrong with that.

Vo•cab•u•lary

accolades (AK koh laydz) awards

Yeah, you know, kids do see bad things when it comes to art and media, but that don't necessarily make them bad people in the end.

Censorship is bad because you have people censoring people, and what do they know?

M: What is the biggest <u>misconception</u> about being Ice Cube and who are some of the big influences on your film career?

The biggest misconception is that I am just Ice Cube. Ice Cube is my ego. Ice Cube's my nickname. People real close to me don't call me Ice Cube, you know what I mean?

So, always the misconception is, you know, I am what I put out only. I am not saying that's not a part of me. It is, but it's not the only part of me. It's the part that I have to put out, you know. So, that's the biggest misconception.

Influences as far as my film career, people like John Singleton, he directed *Boyz in the Hood, Shaft,* and *2 Fast 2 Furious.* He put me in my first movie. He told me to write movies. He said, "You can write a rap, you can write a movie." That kind of opened up a door in my head; I never even thought about it like that, you know. So, he is a big influence on me. He is the one who planted the seed in me that's kind of grown into what it is now. He is the one that I give all the credit to when it comes to my film career. That's where it started. **3**

3 Distinguishing Fact from Opinion Which part of Ice Cube's response contains facts?

A: All right. So, growing up, was there any one experience that really shaped or influenced your life?

I had a half-sister who got killed in 1981. And I was just 12, so that was my wake-up call in life, and what it is really about, you know.

Gotta prevent stuff from happening to you. You know, that's

Vo•cab•u•lary

misconception (mis kuhn SEP shun) a misunderstanding

what youngsters and adults have to think about. Not "Oh, if this happens I'm going to do this," but preventing it from happening to you. So, you have to be alert about your life and which way it is going.

A: I'm a real bookaholic and read all the time. My favorite book so far is *The Human Stain* by Philip Roth or perhaps *Crime and Punishment*. What are a couple of books you think every teenager should read?

You know, I'm more of a pick-up-the-newspaper kind of guy. You know, a *Newsweek, Time* magazine type of guy. I think reading is important in any form. I think a person who's trying to learn to like reading should start off reading about a topic they are interested in, or a person they are interested in.

One of the first books I ever read was *The Autobiography of Malcolm X*. I read it because I had heard about him so much, and I wanted to know who this dude was. So, it was something I was interested in, and it kept me reading.

The key is to find something that clicks in you and makes you love to read. So start off with the thing you are interested in. I mean if you like sports, go get the sports pages and read up on what happened last night. Read about it instead of letting the ESPN man tell you what happened. That's going to get you used to liking reading. ○

Answering the BIG Question

When you do the following activities, consider the Big Question:
Who influences us and how do they do so?

WRITE TO LEARN List the influences in Ice Cube's life and their impact on him in your Learner's Notebook.

PARTNER TALK Join with a classmate who has read this selection. Take turns playing the role of reporter and celebrity. Interview each other about the people who have had the strongest influence on you.

third down and forever

★ ★ ★ ★ ★ ★ ★ ★ ★ ★ ★

When your future's at stake, can you find the courage to speak up for yourself?

by Douglas Holgate

"HEY KIDDO, YOU PLAYED A GREAT GAME TODAY."

"NOTHING LIKE A FOURTH-QUARTER COMEBACK HUH? SIGN OF A TRUE CHAMPION!"

"ESPECIALLY IN A BIG CONFERENCE GAME LIKE THAT."

"THANKS DAD. YEAH IT WAS OKAY... THOUGH WE WOULDN'T HAVE BEEN IN THAT SITUATION IF I WAS CONCENTRATING."

"I SHOULD HAVE LOOKED OFF PAT MORE ON THAT THIRD-QUARTER INTERCEPTION."

"...AND I HADN'T COUNTED ON THE BLITZ COMING AT ME FROM THE LEFT SIDE SO IT HURRIED MY THROW A LITTLE."

"...IT WAS PRETTY BASIC STUFF."

YEAH, BUT YOU PULLED IT OUT IN THE END. AND THAT'S WHAT COUNTS, RIGHT?

215

I'M PROBABLY NOT EVEN THAT GOOD...

...SO LET'S STOP TALKING ABOUT IT!!!

HE GAVE YOU THE "GRAB THE BULL BY THE HORNS," "OPPORTUNITY ONLY COMES ALONG ONCE," TALK AGAIN, DIDN'T HE?

OH BOY. DID YOU TELL HIM ABOUT THE FLYERS?

...NOT YET.

MAN...WHAT IS *WRONG* WITH YOU?! YOU'RE BIGGER AND BETTER THAN "HARDWARE GUY"...

YOU KNOW IT. I KNOW IT.

I KNOW I KNOW! I JUST FEEL BAD, OKAY? HE'S GOT ALL THESE PLANS THAT HE'S BEEN LOOKING FORWARD TO FOR YEARS!

...AND TELLING HIM "BAD LUCK DAD, I DON'T WANT TO FOLLOW YOUR DREAM BECAUSE I WANT TO GO STUDY SOMETHING YOU FIND COMPLETELY POINTLESS," ISN'T EXACTLY GOING TO CUT IT!

I DON'T THINK HE'D EVEN GO FOR ME PLAYING FOOTBALL IN COLLEGE, LET ALONE STUDYING ART!

HMM, THIS CERTAINLY IS ONE OF LIFE'S GREAT BRAIN-TEASERS.

COME ON. LETS GO GET A SODA OR SOMETHING...I HAVE TO GET HOME SOON FOR DINNER.

HEY! CAN I LOOK AT YOUR SKETCHBOOK AGAIN WHEN WE GET THERE?

219

1993...

WOW! YOU'RE A GREAT DRAWER. YOU COULD BE FAMOUS ONE DAY!

THANKS!

1996...

I RECKON YOU'LL EVEN BE GOOD ENOUGH TO DRAW *HULK* ONE DAY!

I'D PREFER BATMAN!

1998...

DANG! HOW DO YOU MAKE IT SO LIFELIKE?!

1999...

I CAN SEE YOUR WORK HANGING HERE ONE DAY, MAN!

TRUST ME.

2001...

DUDE, HOW *CRAZY* WAS JACKSON POLLOCK?

MENTAL. BUT BRILLIANT!

2003...

IF I BEAT YOU, YOU TALK TO MR. PARKS!

NEVER!

TODAY...

SO YOU *SEE*. I'M LIKE SOME KIND OF UNCEASING MOTIVATIONAL DOOM ROBOT! YOU JUST *CAN'T* WIN.

AH HECK. IT'S ALMOST 6:30. I BETTER HEAD HOME. I'LL SEE YOU TOMORROW, MAN!

CHANGING THE SUBJECT WILL GET YOU *NOWHERE*, HUMAN! BEGONE FROM MY SIGHT!

221

THE NEXT DAY...

OKAY – HIT THE CHANGE ROOM BOYS! *GREAT* PRACTICE!

DON'T FORGET. WE HAVE ANOTHER BIG GAME THIS WEEKEND.

AND I'VE ALSO BEEN TOLD THERE WILL BE SOME SCOUTS IN THE CROWD, SO SOME BIG INCENTIVES TO REALLY PLAY WELL.

JUST DO IT SHAUN!!!

HEH. YOU'RE CRAZY MAN.

HEY!

WHAT ARE YA? CHICKEN?!

WHATS THAT GUY'S PROBLEM!? HE'S LUCKY WE DON'T GO UP THERE. *DISRESPECT* MAN. I CAN'T STAND IT!

GEEZ PAT, LEAVE HIM ALONE. HE'S JUST KIDDING AROUND.

DUDE, WHY ARE YOU EVEN *FRIENDS* WITH THAT GUY?

EXACTLY! LISTEN TO KANOA! YOU'RE POPULAR, MAN, YOU CAN HANG OUT WITH ANYONE!

BUT YOU CHOOSE TO HANG OUT WITH *HIM!?*

DOOMBOT COMMANDS IT!

BACK OFF PAT! YOU DON'T EVEN KNOW HIM!

YEAH? WELL I KNOW HE'S A LOSER. AND ONLY LOSERS HANG OUT WITH LOSERS. SO ENJOY!

YEAH... WHATEVER.

222 **UNIT 4** Who influences us and how do they do so?

AND I WONDER WHY I QUESTION DOING THIS INSTEAD OF HELPING OUT MY DAD?

HOLA SEÑOR!! WHAT DO YOU THINK OF MY POSTERS??

YOU LIKE THAT THING AT THE BOTTOM? IT'S A *FIGHTING MUDCAT!!!*

I LOVE THEM. THE OTHER GUYS? NOT SO MUCH.

BAH! THEY WOULDN'T KNOW ART IF IT KICKED THEM IN THE FACE.

YOU *DO* REALIZE THOUGH THAT A 'FIGHTING MUDCAT' IS A CAT*FISH.* NOT A CAT WITH BOXING GLOVES COVERED IN DIRT?

WHAT?! NO! YOU'RE KIDDING, RIGHT?

DO YOU THINK THAT'S WHY THEY DIDN'T LIKE MY POSTER?

HAH! YEAH, MAN – I WOULDN'T BE SURPRISED.

ANYWAY! YOU GOT YOUR STUFF? LET'S GO CHECK OUT WHAT'S ON AT THE MOVIES.

COOL! I GOTTA GO CHANGE. MEET YOU BACK HERE IN ABOUT TEN MINUTES?

WORD!

WHAT KIND OF MASCOT IS A CATFISH ANYWAY?!

BANG!

TWEET!

HOME P 10 ON 2 DOWN 4 YDS TO GO 2 GUESTS 23 QTR 4

THAT'S THE GAME, BOYS!

"WELL THAT'S THAT THEN. I GUESS DAD WAS RIGHT. JUST A HOBBY. NO WAY I'M GETTING ANYWHERE WITH A LOSS..."

"...SO NOW I DON'T EVEN HAVE FOOTBALL TO FALL BACK ON. LOOKS LIKE IT'S BUSINESS SCHOOL AND HARDWARE FROM NOW ON, BUDDY!"

"CONGRATULATIONS!"

MR. THOMAS?

HI... MY NAME IS JOHN FRANKS, I'M WITH MIDWAY U.

YOU PLAYED A GREAT GAME OUT THERE TODAY. YOU SHOULD BE PROUD. YOU REALLY HELD THE TEAM TOGETHER.

OH...THANKS. SORRY I COULDN'T HOLD THEM TOGETHER FOR A WIN.

OH, I'M NOT REALLY CONCERNED WITH THE RESULT, SON.

WHAT I AM IMPRESSED WITH IS YOUR COMPOSURE AND ATTITUDE UNDER THAT PRESSURE.

SO MUCH SO THAT I'D LIKE TO GIVE YOU SOME INFORMATION ON WHAT MIDWAY HAS TO OFFER YOU.

OH!

"I THINK YOU COULD HAVE A REALLY GREAT FUTURE WITH US."

MIDWAY U
The finest arts curriculum in the country

Education Excellence Experience

"...AND IF YOU WOULDN'T MIND, I'D LIKE TO COME AROUND AND ALSO HAVE A CHAT WITH YOUR PARENTS ABOUT EVERYTHING THAT'S INVOLVED."

S...SURE!

LATER THAT EVENING...

"BAD LUCK ABOUT THE GAME, SHAUN. IT'S NEVER FUN TO LOSE THE CLOSE ONES."

"THANKS DAD. I'M NOT TOO UPSET, I PLAYED OKAY. THAT'S WHAT MATTERS RIGHT?"

"WELL, THAT'S RIGHT, BUT LUCKY IT'S ONLY A GAME, HUH? IMAGINE IF IT WAS SOMETHING IMPORTANT YOU LOST?"

"WELL, ACTUALLY DAD, THERE IS SOMETHING REALLY IMPORTANT I'D LIKE TO TALK TO YOU ABOUT."

I'VE GOT A SPREADSHEET OF THE STORE'S SALES OVER THE LAST MONTH OR SO SINCE I STARTED DROPPING FLYERS I DESIGNED INTO PEOPLE'S MAILBOXES...

WE'VE HAD A REVENUE INCREASE OF FIFTY PERCENT, DAD!

OH MY! SHAUN, WHY DIDN'T YOU TELL ME? THIS IS FANTASTIC! NOW I KNOW WHY I'VE BEEN SO RUSHED OFF MY FEET LATELY.

I GUESS THIS ART HOBBY ISN'T SO CRAZY AFTER ALL, HUH?

WELL DONE, SON. THANK YOU.

COULD YOU PASS THE POTATOES, LOVE? THANKS.

KNOCK *KNOCK* *KNOCK*

WHO ON EARTH IS THAT? ARE WE EXPECTING ANYONE?

MUM, DAD? THAT'S DEFINITELY OPPORTUNITY KNOCKING.

END.

WRITE TO LEARN
Who has a stronger influence in your life: your friends or your parents? In your Learner's Notebook, write about which group influences you more and why.

DEALING WITH

PEER

PRESSURE

by Kevin Took, M.D.

Peer pressure: Can you turn it around?

"**C**ome on! ALL of us are cutting math. Who wants to go take that quiz? We're going to take a walk and get lunch instead. Let's go!" says the coolest kid in your class. Do you do what you know is right and go to math class, quiz and all? Or do you give in and go with them?

As you grow older, you'll be faced with some challenging decisions. Some don't have a clear right or wrong answer—like should you play soccer or field hockey? Other decisions involve serious moral questions, like whether to cut class, try cigarettes, or lie to your parents.

Making decisions on your own is hard enough, but when other people get involved and try to pressure you one way or another it can be even harder. People who are your age, like your classmates, are called peers. When they try to influence how you act, to get you to do something, it's called peer pressure. It's something everyone has to deal with—even adults. Let's talk about how to handle it. **1**

1 Identifying Author's Purpose
Why did the author write this article?

Defining Peer Pressure

Peers influence your life, even if you don't realize it, just by spending time with you. You learn from them, and they learn from you. It's only human nature to listen to and learn from other people in your age group.

Peers can have a positive influence on each other. Maybe another student in your science class taught you an easy way to remember the planets in the solar system, or someone on the soccer team taught you a cool trick with the ball. You might admire a friend who is always a good sport and try to be more like him or her. Maybe you got others excited about your new favorite book, and now everyone's reading it. These are examples of how peers positively influence each other every day.

Sometimes peers influence each other in negative ways. For example, a few kids in school might try to get you to cut class with them, your soccer friend might try to convince you to be mean to another player and never pass her the ball, or a kid in

the neighborhood might want you to shoplift with him.

Why Do People Give In to Peer Pressure?

Some kids give in to peer pressure because they want to be liked, to fit in, or because they worry that other kids may make fun of them if they don't go along with the group. Others may go along because they are curious to try something new that others are doing. The idea that "everyone's doing it" may influence some kids to leave their better judgment, or their common sense, behind.

How to Walk Away from Peer Pressure

It is tough to be the only one who says "no" to peer pressure, but you can do it. Paying attention to your own feelings and beliefs about what is right and wrong can help you know the right thing to do. Inner strength and self-confidence can help you stand firm, walk away, and resist doing something when you know better.

It can really help to have at least one other peer, or friend, who is willing to say "no," too. This takes a lot of the power out of peer pressure and makes it much easier to resist. It's great to have friends with values similar to yours who will back you up when you don't want to do something. **2**

You've probably had a parent or teacher advise you to "choose your friends wisely." Peer pressure is a big reason why they say this. If you choose friends who don't use drugs, cut class, smoke cigarettes, or lie to their

> **2 Distinguishing Fact from Opinion**
> Is most of this article based on fact or opinion?

parents, then you probably won't do these things either, even if other kids do. ❸ Try to help a friend who's having trouble resisting peer pressure. It can be powerful for one kid to join another by simply saying, "I'm with you—let's go."

> ❸ **Analyzing Persuasive Techniques**
> How does the writer try to convince you to resist peer pressure?

Even if you're faced with peer pressure while you're alone, there are still things you can do. You can simply stay away from peers who pressure you to do stuff you know is wrong. You can tell them "no" and walk away. Better yet, find other friends and classmates to pal around with.

If you continue to face peer pressure and you're finding it difficult to handle, talk to someone you trust. Don't feel guilty if you've made a mistake or two. Talking to a parent, teacher, or school counselor can help you feel much better and prepare you for the next time you face peer pressure.

Powerful, Positive Peer Pressure

Peer pressure is not always a bad thing. For example, positive peer pressure can be used to pressure bullies into acting better toward other kids. If enough kids get together, peers can pressure each other into doing what's right! ○

Answering the BIG Question

When you do the following activities, consider the Big Question:
Who influences us and how do they do so?

WRITE TO LEARN Think of a time you were positively influenced by a peer. Think of a time someone tried to pressure you into doing something you shouldn't. Write a paragraph in your Learner's Notebook explaining each situation and how you handled it.

PARTNER TALK Meet with a classmate who has read this selection. Share your ideas of how peer pressure can be a positive thing.

Thanking the Birds

by Joseph Bruchac

Share an Apache man's wisdom about the gifts of the earth.

One day 30 years ago, Swift Eagle, an <u>Apache</u> man, visited some friends on the Onondaga Indian Reservation in central New York. While he was out walking, he heard sounds of boys playing in the bushes.

"There's another one. Shoot it!" said one of the boys.

When he pushed through the brush to see what was happening, he found that they had been shooting small birds with a BB gun. They had already killed a chickadee, a robin, and several blackbirds. The boys looked up at him, uncertain what he was going to do or say.

There are several things that a non-Indian bird lover might have done: given a stern lecture on the evil of killing birds; threatened to tell the boys' parents on them for doing something they had been told not to do; or even spanked them. Swift Eagle, however, did something else.

"Ah," he said, "I see you have been hunting. Pick up your game and come with me."

Vo•cab•u•lary

Apache (uh PA chee) a member of a group of Native American peoples of the southwestern United States

231

He led the boys to a place where they could make a fire and cook the birds. He made sure they said a "thank you" to the spirits of the birds before eating them, and as they ate he told stories. It was important, he said, to be thankful to the birds for the gifts of their songs, their feathers, and their bodies as food. The last thing he said to them they never forgot—for it was one of those boys who told me this story many years later: "You know, our Creator gave the gift of life to everything that is alive. Life is a very sacred thing. But our Creator knows that we have to eat to stay alive. That is why it is permitted to hunt to feed ourselves and our people. So I understand that you boys must have been very, very hungry to kill those little birds." ❶

I have always liked that story, for it illustrates several things. Although there was a wide range of customs, life-ways, and languages—in pre-Columbian times more than 400 different languages were spoken on the North American continent—many close similarities existed between virtually all of the Native American peoples. Thus ideas held by an Apache from the Southwest fitted into the lives and traditions of Onondagas in the Northeast.

> ❶ **Analyzing Persuasive Techniques**
> How does Swift Eagle persuade the boys to change their ways?

Vo•cab•u•lary

pre-Columbian (pree cuh LUHM bee uhn) before Columbus arrived in America

One of these ideas, expressed in Swift Eagle's words to the boys, was the continent-wide belief that mankind depended on the natural world for survival, on the one hand, and had to respect it and remain in right relationship with it, on the other...

As the <u>anecdote</u> about Swift Eagle also shows, the children were taught the values of their culture through example and stories. Instead of scolding or lecturing them, Swift Eagle showed the boys how to build a fire and cook the game they had shot, giving the songbirds the same respect he would have given a rabbit or deer. He told stories that pointed out the value of those birds as living beings.

The <u>ritual</u> activity of making the fire, thanking the spirit of the birds, hearing the stories, and then eating the game they had killed taught the boys more than a hundred stern lectures would have done, and the lesson stayed with them all their lives. ❷ ○

> ❷ **Distinguishing Fact from Opinion**
> Is this statement about the boys a fact, or is it the author's opinion?

Answering the BIG Question

When you do the following activities, consider the Big Question:
Who influences us and how do they do so?

WRITE TO LEARN How did Swift Eagle try to change the boys' minds about hunting birds? Do you think they learned their lesson? Write down your answers in your Learner's Notebook.

LITERATURE GROUPS Join with two or three classmates who have read the selection. Talk about a time when an adult influenced your behavior and how he or she did it.

Vo·cab·u·lary

anecdote (AN eck doht) a short, amusing story
ritual (RICH oo uhl) according to religious law or social custom

Whose REALITY Are We Talking About?

When it comes to TV, what is reality anyway?

Have you ever wondered if what you witness on reality TV happened the way it's shown? How do the producers manage to fit comedy, romance, and drama all into one episode? And why are women on most reality television shows thin and universally "cute" when they are supposed to be average people? And do these shows represent the racial and class diversity of the U.S.—NOT! We think reality TV has a big problem living up to its name.

"Starving to Make the Final Cut"
Madia Campagna, 13, California

"America is not ready for a plus-size model," Nolé Marin says to the other judges on an episode of *America's Next Top Model*. Have you ever wondered why practically everyone on television and on the covers of teen magazines is very thin? ❶ Why do you suppose the producers put skinny actors and

> ❶ **Identifying Author's Perspective**
> Do you agree with what the author says about models?

models in shows and in magazines if they do not look like the average woman?

Women in the United States are under pressure to obtain a certain social and cultural ideal of beauty, which can lead to their own poor body image. The media suggests that only a slender woman's figure is beautiful—well, there are other body types in the real world.

America's Next Top Model sends messages that suggest the only way to become a model is to eat meals of just vegetables. You practically have to starve in order to be a contestant on the show. *America's Next Top Model* should find more contestants with a sense of style and creativity, and producers should not cut everyone out of the show who weighs over 140 pounds.

By featuring women of all body types, more girls who are not skinny could have a shot at becoming *America's Next Top Model* and adolescents would have better feelings about their bodies. I dare magazines and directors of shows to hire participants who are average adolescents for a chance to prove that we are more than just how we look.

"Real Fake TV"
Karyn Wight, 16, Massachusetts

Have you ever noticed just how fake reality TV is? The producers totally cut out what really happens and they only show you when people are acting stupid and making complete fools of themselves. Take *The Bachelor* for example; totally unrealistic. How can one man fall in love with one woman when he is dating ten others as well? Love should happen gradually and progress over time; it should not be set up in a romance that probably won't last.

America's Next Top Model is so fake. These women are so self-centered that it makes my stomach hurt. The producers give women a bad image of being vindictive and ruthless, willing to do anything and go to any measure to reach the top. I just think that reality TV is such a waste of time and I wish people could see how phony it is. **2**

2 Distinguishing Fact from Opinion
How do you know that this paragraph is an opinion?

"Pretty in Plastic"
Kenza Guessous, California

The Swan, a plastic surgery reality show on FOX, introduces you to average women who are transformed into "drop dead gorgeous" women with plastic surgery. The women notice the façade that surgery has created, which masks their prior appearances.

The FOX network has a large teen audience, many of whom watch *The Swan*. Watching this show might contribute to teenagers wanting plastic surgery. ❸ Teenagers may become obsessive and want to continue transforming their image. In shows like *The Swan*, the producers are very biased because they only present the positive aspects of surgery. Plastic surgery may solve some "problems," but it will not change who you are on the inside.

> ❸ **Comparing and Contrasting**
> How does this author's viewpoint compare to that of the author on page 235?

Before one chooses to have plastic surgery, you must know the risks. Is life worth risking on an unpredictable procedure? If the surgery is successful, what do you gain? Before deciding to get plastic surgery, you should consider all the consequences and risks you are taking. ○

Answering the BIG Question

When you do the following activities, consider the Big Question:
Who influences us and how do they do so?

WRITE TO LEARN Write a brief entry in your Learner's Notebook about how the selections influenced your thoughts about reality TV. Do you agree or disagree with the points presented? Why?

LITERATURE GROUPS Get together with two or three classmates who have read the selections. Discuss your opinions with a group.

A Gold Miner's Tale

by Bobbi Katz

Water and sand—could that really be all it takes to get fabulously rich?

Frank Wexler
Dawson City, Yukon Territory, 1898

I was twenty-one years old.
Fired up by dreams of gold.
Rushing West in '49
To stake a claim to my own mine!
What did I find when I got there?
Thousands of "<u>rushers</u>" everywhere!
Water and sand. That's ALL it takes.
Swish your pan. Pick out the <u>flakes</u>!

A meal?
A horse?
A place to stay?
Who'd believe what we had to pay!
Bought a shovel. Bought a pan.

Vo•cab•u•lary

rushers (RUH sherz) people who traveled to California in pursuit of gold
flakes (flayks) gold flakes

Soon I'd be a rich young man.
Water and sand. That's ALL it takes.
Swish your pan. Pick out the flakes!
Pan after pan. I'd swish and wish
For a glint of pay dirt in my dish.
Asleep at night, what did I see?
Nuggets the daylight hid from me.
It takes more than a flash in the pan
To make a rusher a rich young man.

The gold I found? Just enough to get by.
I gave up when my claim went dry.
Water and sand. That's ALL it takes.
Swish your pan. Pick out the flakes!
Got a job in a <u>hydraulic mine</u>.
Hated the work, but the pay was fine.
So when I heard about <u>Pikes Peak</u>,
I was in the Rockies within a week!

Vo·cab·u·lary

hydraulic (hy DRAW lik) **mine** a process of mining using water
Pikes Peak (PYKS peek) mountain located near Colorado Springs, Colorado

Water and sand. That's ALL it takes.
Swish your pan. Pick out the flakes!
I should have known better.
With a grubstake so small,
I left Colorado with nothing at all.
No job. No gold. Just a shovel and a pan.
But I walked away a wiser man. **1**

"Gold in the Klondike!"
Wouldn't you think
I'd be up there in a wink?
But with my new plan to pan gold flakes,
I didn't make the same mistakes.
Before I joined the great stampede,
I thought: What will stampeders need?
Now I'm a Dawson millionaire!
I sell them ALL long underwear. O

1 Comparing and Contrasting
How did the miner's experience contrast with his expectation?

Answering the BIG Question

When you do the following activities, consider the Big Question:
Who influences us and how do they do so?

WRITE TO LEARN How is the speaker in the poem influenced by others? Why does he follow them West and to Pikes Peak? What does he learn from his experiences? Write a brief paragraph in your Learner's Notebook that answers these questions.

PARTNER TALK The speaker in the poem turned a disappointment into an opportunity. Discuss with a partner a real or imaginary situation in which you could do the same thing.

Vo•cab•u•lary

grubstake (GRUHB stayk) money given to a miner to fund his trip in exchange for sharing the profits of his discoveries

JIMMY JET AND HIS TV SET

by Shel Silverstein

Poor Jimmy Jet is so influenced by TV that the unthinkable happens.

I'll tell you the story of Jimmy Jet—
And you know what I tell you is true.
He loved to watch his TV set
Almost as much as you.

He watched all day, he watched all night
Till he grew pale and lean,
From "The Early Show" to "The Late Late Show"
And all the shows between.

He watched till his eyes were frozen wide,
And his bottom grew into his chair.
And his chin turned into a tuning dial,
And antennae grew out of his hair.

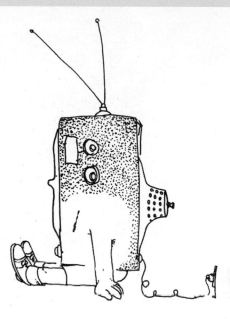

And his brains turned into TV tubes,
And his face to a TV screen.
And two knobs saying "VERT." and "HORIZ."
Grew where his ears had been. ❶

And he grew a plug that looked like a tail
So we plugged in little Jim.
And now instead of him watching TV
We all sit around and watch him. ⊙

❶ **Identifying Author's Purpose**
Why do you think this poet wrote this poem?

Answering the BIG Question

When you do the following activities, consider the Big Question:
Who influences us and how do they do so?

WRITE TO LEARN Watching too much TV can affect a person's health. Write a brief entry in your Learner's Notebook answering the question: How can watching TV negatively affect your health?

PARTNER TALK Meet with a classmate who has read the selection. Discuss your entries and the ways in which TV affects your lives.

FROM

WAITING
FOR WAR
THE

by Graham Salisbury

**Two young men reach out across cultures, but one of them may
soon be facing his own death.**

---

*A young Hawaiian boy named Henry has just bought a horse.
He can't ride the horse, and now he begins to wonder why he bought
it. In addition, Henry must pay for the horse's upkeep. To earn
money, Henry and his friend Sammy hop on a bus to Hotel Street in
downtown Honolulu where they shine shoes. On the bus, Henry and
Sammy meet an American soldier.*

Every bus at every stop on every day was always sweaty
full. But they squeezed onto it anyway, rode standing up, packing
in like Vienna sausages. Mostly local people were on it, but there
were also some war workers and a few military guys, who all
looked young, some almost as young as Henry and Sammy.

One guy on the bus was crammed up close to Henry. He was
snappy clean in his khaki uniform. Army guy, probably from
Schofield. Henry liked his hat, tilted to the side like it was. The
guy caught Henry looking and dipped his chin, Hello.

Henry turned away.

Later Henry glanced at him again. He guessed the guy was probably about nineteen. He had dark hair, almost black. And blue eyes. Henry hadn't seen that very often, black hair and blue eyes.

"Howdy," the army guy said to Henry. The guy was just trying to be friendly.

Henry didn't know what to do.

"My name's Mike," the guy said.

Sammy, who was standing right behind Henry, let out a small scoffing sound that said, *Can you believe this joker is talking to us?*

Henry looked down at his feet.

They rode for thirty minutes more in silence. Once the driver stopped the bus and got out and smoked a cigarette. The drivers did things like that because they had so many customers they didn't care anymore how they treated them, and everyone waited on the bus, afraid to get off and lose their place. When he was done, the driver got back on and continued on toward Honolulu.

Half the people on the bus got off on Hotel Street, Henry and Sammy among them. And Mike, who went off by himself. Funny he was by himself, Henry thought. Mostly those guys went around in packs.

"He likes you," Sammy whispered.

"Shuddup. You're sick, you know? You need help."

"Yeah, yeah."

They walked around. It was hot, the street sending up as much heat as the sun. Every place you looked was jammed with uniforms, white for navy, khaki for army, everywhere.

"Let's go check out the tattoo shops," Sammy said.

"Which ones? There must be fifty of them."

"All of them got Filipino artists," Sammy said. "You know,

Vo·cab·u·lary

scoffing (SKAWF ing) mocking

sometimes they do five hundred tattoos a day. You know what's the most popular? *Remember Pearl Harbor.*"

"How do you know that?"

"I know."

"Shh. You so full of it, Sammy."

"No. It's true. My uncle told me that."

He was probably right, since Sammy had Filipino blood. ❶

"Hey," Henry said, "how about Savage?"

"What?"

"The horse. Call him Savage."

"Junk," Sammy said. "How 'bout <u>Spats</u>?"

"Spats?"

"He got a white foot."

"But he only has one."

"So?"

"So you gotta call him Spat, then. Not Spats."

Sammy frowned. "Sound like somebody spit something."

"The no-name horse."

Sammy said, "What did Wong call it?"

"The horse."

Sammy shook his head. "I still like Bucky."

A fight broke out in front of a bar. Men yelling and shoving. Henry and Sammy ran over to see. A war worker and a navy guy were going at it, but two navy SPs broke it up before it got any farther. The war worker guy went off looking back and swearing at the navy guy, telling him he better watch his back.

> ❶ **Distinguishing Fact from Opinion**
> Does Sammy's Filipino blood make his statement about tattoos a fact?

Vo·cab·u·lary

spats (spats) cloth or leather covers for the upper part of a shoe and ankle

"Look," Henry said.

Sammy turned around.

Mike.

Mike smiled when he saw them and came over, saying, "Not much of a fight, huh?"

Henry still didn't know what to do around Mike, or any service guy who was by himself. He sure didn't want to talk to him. But he did wonder where he was from. Ohio, probably. Or maybe Iowa. They were all from places like that—at least that's what his father told him. "From Ohio to the grave," he'd said. "So sad. They're just kids. Farmers and grocery-store stock boys. Come way out here to fight and die."

But Henry never thought about that. He didn't care where they were from. He just knew he didn't like them. Like the rest of his friends.

"Uh . . . yeah," Henry said. "The SPs broke it up."

"So," Mike said, then said no more.

Sammy turned to walk away.

Henry wanted to go, too, but the guy was just trying to be friendly and, well, he wasn't so bad. Henry grabbed Sammy's arm. "Wait."

Sammy stopped and turned back quickly, like maybe Henry was going to fight the guy.

Henry searched for something to say. Nothing came.

"I hate this street," Mike said. "Nothing's real, you know? Don't it seem that way to you?"

Sammy tugged at Henry's arm, like, *Come on, let's get out of here already. We got shoes to shine.*

"Yeah," Henry said to the army guy. "But it's kind of fun to watch all you guys stand around waiting."

Mike shook his head. "That's what we do, ain't it? Wait. Wait for everything. Wait for a cup of coffee. Wait for a shoeshine. Wait for the war."

Henry hadn't ever thought of that before, wait for the war. Strange.

Sammy turned his back to them.

"What's your name?" the army guy, Mike, asked.

"Henry. And this is Sammy," he added, pointing a thumb back over his shoulder.

Finally Sammy turned around. He nodded, but coldly, like maybe he'd rather spit than talk. ❷

"He's not as bad as he looks," Henry said, grinning.

Mike put out his hand to shake.

Henry hesitated but shook. The guy's grip was strong. That was good.

> ❷ **Comparing and Contrasting**
> How are Henry's and Sammy's reactions to Mike different?

Sammy shook, too, <u>reluctantly</u>, and Henry prayed to heaven that his father wasn't watching from some secret hole in the wall.

"Where you from?" Henry asked, and Sammy threw his head back as if to say, *Jeez, you gotta be kidding, come on, let's go.*

"Tyler, Texas. Ever heard of it?"

"No. But I heard of Texas."

Mike nodded, then dipped his head toward the rope hanging out of Henry's pocket. "What's the rope for?"

Henry turned to look. He'd forgotten all about it. "Uh . . . oh, that. I got a horse. Me and Sammy was riding it today."

Sammy <u>stifled</u> a laugh.

"No kidding," Mike said. "What kind of horse is it?"

"A brown one."

"A brown one?"

Vo·cab·u·lary

reluctantly (rih LUK tunt lee) unwillingly
stifled (STY fuld) held back

"Yeah, brown."

Mike scratched the back of his head and thought a moment. "You think . . ." He paused, thought some more. "You . . . you think I could ride your horse? I ain't seen mine in six months."

That woke Sammy up. He grinned. "Sure, you can ride it," he said.

Henry said, "He's kind of . . . well, he don't let nobody ride him but me." The last thing he wanted was to have this _haole_ messing up his horse. And if his father ever heard of it, he'd—

"Got him trained, huh?" Mike said.

Sammy laughed.

"What?" Mike asked. "You boys pulling my leg?"

"No-no," Henry said. "I really got a horse. It's just . . . hard to ride, that's all."

"Yeah, hard to ride," Sammy added. "We can't even catch it."

Henry thought, _We?_

"Bet he'd let me on him," Mike said.

"How much?" Sammy asked.

"What do you mean?" Mike said.

"You said you bet. How much?"

Mike grinned. "Okay. How much you got?"

That stopped Sammy, who was broke as a lizard. He waved Mike off, as if to say, _Forget it already._

"Tell you what," Mike said. "If I can't ride the horse, I'll give each of you five bucks. But if I _can_ ride him, then you let me visit him once in a while. How's that?"

"You got a deal," Sammy said, sticking out his hand to shake.

"Hey," Henry said. "It's not your horse to bet."

Vo·cab·u·lary

haole (HOW lee) a Hawaiian word for foreigner; here it means a white person

"Sure it is," Sammy said. "I'm the trainer."

Okay, Henry thought. *Fine.* What did he have to lose, anyway? If he got five bucks from Mike, the horse would be free. He shook hands with Mike. "Let's go, then."

Mike grinned. "Now you're talkin'."

The horse was way over on the far side of the field, standing in the blue shade of a <u>mango</u> tree. The air was still, no breeze, no cars or people around. Henry, Sammy, and Mike leaned against the rotting wood fence, batting flies away from their faces, studying the horse.

"He ain't a purebred or anything," Mike said. "But he don't look bad. Nice lines, nice head. He got a name?" ❸

❸ **Distinguishing Fact from Opinion**
Are Mike's comments about the horse a fact or an opinion?

"Bucky."

"Not Bucky," Henry said, shoving Sammy. "He don't have a name yet. I'm still thinking about it."

"How long you had the horse?" Mike asked.

"A week."

Mike nodded. "Let's go take a look."

Mike stepped up and over the fence. Henry and Sammy followed him into the pasture, single file.

On the other side, the horse stood staring at them, head up, ears cocked forward. When they got about halfway across, the horse bolted and trotted down to the lower corner.

Mike stopped and looked around. About two acres of grass and weeds. A few trees. He turned to the pond near the lower end where the horse was now. "How deep is the water?"

Henry shrugged. "I don't know. Five or six feet. In the middle.

Vo·cab·u·lary

mango (MAYN goh) a tropical Asian evergreen tree grown for its sweet fruit

I don't think it's any deeper than that."

Sammy said, "You got two five buckses on you?"

Mike pulled out a small folded wad of bills, and Sammy's eyes grew into plates. "Don't you worry, I got it. But the thing is, I'm keeping it, because me and that horse down there are going to get along just fine."

Sammy grinned. "That's what you think."

Mike said, "Stay close behind me, and walk slow."

The horse raised its head and trotted off a ways. Mike stopped and the horse stopped, looking back at them. With his eyes still on the horse, Mike reached back, saying, "Let me have that rope."

Henry handed him the rope from his back pocket.

Mike let one end of it drop, then looped it back into his hand. "You boys go stand over by the fence."

Henry and Sammy went down to the fence, walking backward. "What are you going do?" Sammy asked.

"Make friends. Talk a little."

"*Talk?*" Sammy <u>snickered</u>, then mumbled to Henry, "You heard that? He going to talk to the horse." He half laughed then glanced back at Mike. "This I gotta see."

"Me too," Henry said. "The guy strange, yeah?"

Mike walked over to the pond. He studied it a moment, then looked up. The horse was on the other side of it now, watching him.

Sammy said, "Pretty soon he going see why we call him Bucky."

Vo•cab•u•lary

snickered (SNIK urd) partly held back a laugh

Mike walked around the pond.

The horse headed away, not running, just keeping a certain distance with one ear cocked back toward Mike. It snorted once and threw its head.

Mike stopped again. This time he looked to the side, not directly at the horse.

The horse stood waiting.

Mike walked away from it. Just kind of strolled off. And the horse took a few steps toward him. Amazing.

Mike stopped.

The horse stopped.

Mike walked, and the horse followed.

This went on for a few minutes until the horse finally walked all the way up to Mike's back. But Mike didn't try to put the rope over his neck. In fact, he didn't even turn around. He just stood with his back to the horse. When the horse was only a couple of feet away, Mike finally turned and faced it. He said something softly. ❹

"What he's saying?" Sammy asked.

"Who knows. Weird, man."

"You telling me."

Mike reached up to put his hand on the horse's nose. And the horse didn't throw his head like he always did when Henry got near him. Mike said something again, and reached into his pocket.

"What's he got? Sammy asked.

Henry didn't answer, too interested in how Mike was taming the horse.

The horse ate whatever it was Mike has in his pocket, and Mike ran his hand along its neck. Then, slowly, he looped the rope around the horse's nose, making a kind of rope bridle. There

❹ **Comparing and Contrasting**
What are some similarities between the way Mike makes friends with the horse and the way he approaches the boys?

was a name for it, but Henry couldn't remember what it was. *Hack* something. Anyway, the horse let Mike do it, just let him.

"Look at that," Henry whispered.

"He still ain't riding it."

Mike led the horse over to the pond, then let the end of the rope fall to the ground. The horse stood still.

Mike took off his shoes and socks. He took off his hat and set it on the shoes. Then his watch.

"What he going do now?" Sammy said. "Go swimming?"

"Shhh. Quiet."

Mike unbuttoned his shirt, took it off. Then his pants and olive-green undershirt. He looked back at Henry and Sammy and grinned.

"Look at that dingdong, standing there in his boxers."

"I think you're right. He's going swimming."

"Man, that guy is white."

"Look like a squid."

Mike led the horse into the pond, talking to it and easing it in slowly. The horse went willingly. No problem. Right in, up to its chest. Mike dipped his hand in the water and scooped up a handful, then let it fall over the horse's back.

"He's giving it a bath," Sammy said.

Henry frowned. What was the guy *doing*?

Then Mike leaned against the horse. Just leaned.

A minute or two later, he threw himself up over its back, so that he lay over it on his stomach, like a blanket. The horse moved but settled down quickly.

"Ahhh," Henry whispered. "The guy is smart, very, very smart. He going get on him in the water, where the horse can't run, or throw him off, or if he does throw him off, going be an easy fall. Smart."

When the horse was settled, Mike eased up on its back and sat, bareback. For a long moment he just sat.

Henry grinned. He liked what he was seeing. Someone could at least get on the horse, even if it was a mainland army guy. Mike was okay. He didn't call anyone "boy" or "native" or complain about where he was. **5**

5 Comparing and Contrasting How is Mike different from other *haoles* Henry has met?

Mike took up the rope bridle and nudged the horse with his heels. The horse jumped, then walked out of the pond. Mike rode around the pond. Rode up to the top of the pasture, then back.

Henry thought Mike looked pretty good on him.

Mike clucked his tongue, and the horse broke into an easy run. Mike rode smoothly on its back, and Henry could hardly believe that someone could ride a horse like that with no saddle and not bounce off.

"I don't believe it," Sammy said.

"The guy knows what he's doing."

"Unlike us."

"Yeah, unlike us."

A few minutes later, Mike rode up. Stopped, sat looking down at them. "This is still a fine horse, Henry. He's a little old, and he hasn't been ridden in a while, but he's been ridden in the past."

"He wouldn't even let me near him."

"You just have to know how to talk to him, that's all."

"Stupid to talk to a horse," Sammy said.

"No, it ain't. It's part of gaining his trust. After that he'll let you ride him."

Sammy frowned.

Henry said, "Well, I guess you won the bet."

"You want to try riding him?"

"Nah."

"Come on. He's your horse."

"It won't let me on it."

"Sure he will." Mike slid off. "Come, stand here by him, let him smell you, let him look at you."

"Uh . . . I don't know," Henry said.

The horse twisted an ear toward him.

"Go ahead," Mike said. "Rub his nose, tell him he's a good horse."

Henry inched closer and rubbed the horse's nose. It was soft, soft as feathers. The eye was big and shiny. Brown. "Nice horse," he said, like you'd say to a dog.

"Good," Mike said, "Here, take the rope. Walk around, let him follow you."

Henry led the horse around the pond.

Mike and Sammy stood silently watching.

Out on the ocean two destroyers and a transport ship were heading away from Pearl Harbor. In the distance you could hear the faint cracking of rifle shots, men maneuvering in the hills. A plane droned by, silver in the clear blue sky. 6

> **6 Identifying Author's Purpose**
> Why does the author mention the war preparations at this point?

When Henry got back Mike said, "Okay, see if you can get on him. If he gets jumpy, you can take him into the water like I did. He likes the water. Come up and lean on his side, let him get used to you. Then try to get up on him."

Henry put his arms over the horse's back and leaned on him. The horse's ears turned back, then forward again.

"See?" Mike said. "Now go on, get on him."

Henry took the rope bridle, grabbed a hank of mane, and jumped up on its back. The horse took a few sidesteps, then settled down. Henry grinned.

Vo·cab·u·lary

maneuvering (muh NOO vur ing) moving as part of a planned military exercise
droned (drohnd) made a low humming sound

"See?" Sammy said. "I told you you could ride it if you were nice to it."

Henry rode the horse to the top of the field, then back down again. "He's really *not* a bad horse," he said when he got back.

"No, he sure ain't," Mike said.

Henry rode around the pond two times, then came back and slid off. He took the rope bridle off and set the horse free. But the horse just stood there.

Mike went down to the pond to get his clothes. He was dry now, from the sun. He got dressed and the three of them walked back over to the road.

Mike said, "So it's okay, then, if I come see the horse?"

"Yeah-yeah," Henry said. "Anytime. Just come see 'um, ride 'um, whatever you want."

Mike grinned and shook hands with Henry and Sammy. "Thanks. I hope I can get up here a couple more times before I ship out."

"Yeah, couple times," Henry said. "Hey, what you had in your pocket, that you gave the horse?"

"Jelly beans."

"Hah," Henry said.

"When he does something right, reward him. Always reward good work, good behavior."

Sammy said, "Like when you guys get a medal, yeah?"

Mike looked down and said, "Yeah, like that. Well . . ." **7**

"Yeah," Henry said.

Mike nodded and waited a moment, then nodded again and started down the road to the bus stop.

"He's not a bad guy," Sammy said. "For a *haole* army guy."

"He sure knows horses."

"Yeah."

7 Comparing and Contrasting
How is a medal awarded in wartime similar to and different from the reward the horse gets for good behavior?

Henry and Sammy were silent a moment. Henry kept thinking of what Mike had said about waiting for the war. Waiting for the war. He'd never thought of it like that before, all of those guys just waiting to go fight. They'd always just been guys causing trouble around town. But, Henry thought, that was nothing next to the trouble they were waiting for.

"He might die soon, you know, Sammy."

Sammy shook his head. "A lot of them don't come back."

For the first time since the bombing of Pearl Harbor, for the first time since the three-day ship fires and massive clouds of dirty smoke and mass burials, for the first time since the arrest of his Japanese friends and neighbors, for the first time since then, Henry thought about how even now, right now, today, guys like Mike were out there somewhere dying in the war, going out on a transport ship and not coming back. Young guys, like him and Sammy. Just kids from Texas.

"I hope he makes it," Henry said.

"Yeah."

"But probably . . ."

In that moment, with those words, Henry changed. He could feel it in his guts, a weird, dark feeling—all those young guys just like him, those guys from the mainland, from farms and towns and cities, coming way out here to wait for the war, to wait, to wait, to wait— then to go. And die. All of them would die, he thought.

Henry winced, then shook his head. He rubbed the back of his neck.

"You know what I going name my horse, Sammy?"

"What."

"Mike."

"Mike?"

"After the guy."

"Yeah," Sammy said. He was quiet a moment, then he said, "Because why?"

"Because that guy . . . he going ship out . . . and he ain't coming back."

"You don't know that."

"One way or the other, Sammy, he ain't coming back."

"What you mean?"

"I mean he going get shot and die. Or he going live through things that going make him feel like he was dead. That's what I think, and it ain't right, you know? It ain't supposed to be that way." **8**

They were both silent for a long while.

Finally Sammy looked back at the horse and said, "Mike."

"Yeah . . . Mike."

The horse took a step forward, grazing. And above the mountains, white clouds slept. ○

8 Identifying Author's Perspective
How does the author feel about war?

Answering the BIG Question

When you do the following activities, consider the Big Question:
Who influences us and how do they do so?

WRITE TO LEARN Think about a time when you may have misjudged someone based on how the person looked or the social group he or she belonged to. Write a brief entry in your Learner's Notebook describing your experience.

LITERATURE GROUPS Mike helps Henry grow. He teaches him how to tame a horse and makes Henry think about what will happen to the young soldiers. Meet with two other students who have read this story. Discuss a time when someone helped you grow in some way. How did you feel about that person?

The Struggle to Be an All-American Girl

by Elizabeth Wong

How far would you go to avoid being different?

*I*t's still there, the Chinese school on Yale Street where my brother and I used to go. Despite the new coat of paint and the high wire fence, the school I knew 10 years ago remains remarkably <u>stoically</u> the same.

Every day at 5 p.m., instead of playing with our fourth- and fifth-grade friends or sneaking out to the empty lot to hunt ghosts and animal bones, my brother and I had to go to Chinese school. No amount of kicking, screaming, or pleading could <u>dissuade</u> my

Vo·cab·u·lary

stoically (STOH ih klee) without showing feeling; in a calm way
dissuade (dih SWAYD) to change someone's mind

mother, who was solidly determined to have us learn the language of our heritage.

Forcibly she walked us the seven long, hilly blocks from our home to school, depositing our defiant tearful faces before the stern principal. My only memory of him is that he swayed on his heels like a palm tree, and he always clasped his impatient twitching hands behind his back. I recognized him as a repressed maniacal child killer, and knew that if we ever saw his hands we'd be in big trouble. ❶ We all sat in little chairs in an empty auditorium. The room smelled like Chinese medicine, an imported faraway mustiness. Like ancient mothballs or dusty closets. I hated that smell. I favored crisp new scents. Like the soft French perfume that my American teacher wore in public school. There was a stage far to the right, flanked by an American flag and the flag of the Nationalist Republic of China, which was also red, white, and blue, but not as pretty.

❶ **Distinguishing Fact from Opinion**
Is the writer stating a fact or voicing an opinion?

Although the emphasis at the school was mainly language—speaking, reading, writing—the lessons always began with an exercise in politeness. With the entrance of the teacher, the best student would tap a bell and everyone would get up, kowtow, and chant, "Sing san ho," the phonetic for "How are you, teacher?" Being 10 years old, I had better things to learn than ideographs copied painstakingly in lines that ran right to left from the tip of a moc but, a real ink pen that had to be held in an awkward way if blotches were to be avoided. After all, I could do the multiplication tables, name the satellites of Mars, and write reports on *Little Women* and *Black Beauty*. Nancy Drew, my

---

Vo•cab•u•lary

forcibly (FOR sih blee) with force
maniacal (muh NY ih kul) mad, crazy
kowtow (KOW tow) to kneel and touch the forehead to the ground in respect
phonetic (foh NET ick) spoken language or speech sounds
ideographs (ID ee oh grafs) symbols for words

favorite book heroine, never spoke Chinese.

The language was a source of embarrassment. More times than not, I had tried to <u>dissociate</u> myself from the nagging loud voice that followed me wherever I wandered in the nearby American supermarket outside Chinatown. The voice belonged to my grandmother, a fragile woman in her 70s who could outshout the best of the street vendors. Her humor was <u>raunchy</u>, her Chinese rhythmless, patternless. It was quick, it was loud, it was unbeautiful. It was not like the quiet, lilting romance of French or the gentle refinement of the American South. Chinese sounded <u>pedestrian</u>. Public.

In Chinatown, the comings and goings of hundreds of Chinese on their daily tasks sounded <u>chaotic</u> and frenzied. I did not want to be thought of as mad, as talking gibberish. When I spoke English, people nodded at me, smiled sweetly, said encouraging words. Even the people in my culture would cluck and say that I'd do well in life. "My, doesn't she move her lips fast," they'd say, meaning that I'd be able to keep up with the world outside Chinatown.

My brother was even more <u>fanatical</u> than I about speaking English. He was especially hard on my mother, criticizing her, often cruelly, for her <u>pidgin</u> speech—smatterings of Chinese scattered like chop suey in her conversation. "It's not 'What it is,' Mom," he'd

Vo·cab·u·lary

dissociate (dis SOH shee ayt) to separate oneself from something
raunchy (RAWN chee) vulgar
pedestrian (puh DES tree en) commonplace, average
chaotic (kay AW tik) confused, unpredictable
fanatical (fuh NAT uh kuhl) excessively devoted
pidgin (PIH jin) simplified, usually mixing words of more than one language

say in <u>exasperation</u>. "It's 'What *is*, what *is*, what *is*!'" Sometimes, Mom might leave out an occasional "the" or "a," or perhaps a verb of being. He would stop her in mid-sentence. "Say it again, Mom. Say it right." When he tripped over his own tongue, he'd blame it on her: "See, Mom, it's all your fault. You set a bad example."

What infuriated my mother most was when my brother cornered her on her consonants, especially "r." My father had played a cruel joke on Mom by assigning her an American name that her tongue wouldn't allow her to say. No matter how hard she tried, "Ruth" always ended up "Luth" or "Roof."

After two years of writing with a *moc but* and reciting words with multiples of meanings, I finally was granted a cultural divorce. I was permitted to stop Chinese school. I thought of myself as multicultural. I preferred tacos to egg rolls; I enjoyed Cinco de Mayo more than Chinese New Year. At last, I was one of you; I wasn't one of them.

Sadly, I still am. ❷ ○

> ❷ **Identifying Author's Perspective**
> How does the author feel about her heritage?

Answering the BIG Question

When you do the following activities, consider the Big Question:
Who influences us and how do they do so?

WRITE TO LEARN Write a paragraph in your Learner's Notebook to answer the following question: What influences in the author's life made her embrace the American culture and deny her Chinese heritage?

PARTNER TALK Share your paragraph with a partner who has read the selection. Discuss how you might feel in Elizabeth's situation.

Vo•cab•u•lary

exasperation (eg zas pur AY shun) annoyance, aggravation

A Crush

by Cynthia Rylant

A secret love causes more than just flowers to blossom.

*W*hen the windows of Stan's Hardware started filling up with flowers, everyone in town knew something had happened. <u>Excess</u> flowers usually mean death, but since these were all real flowers bearing the aroma of nature instead of floral preservative, and since they stood bunched in clear mason jars instead of impaled on Styrofoam crosses, everyone knew nobody had died. So they all figured somebody had a crush and kept quiet.

There wasn't really a Stan of Stan's Hardware. Dick Wilcox was the owner, and since he'd never liked his own name, he gave

Vo·cab·u·lary

excess (EK ses) extra; more than needed

his store half the name of his childhood hero, Stan Laurel in the movies. Dick had been married for twenty-seven years. Once, his wife Helen had dropped a German chocolate cake on his head at a Lion's Club dance, so Dick and Helen were not likely candidates for the honest expression of the flowers in those clear mason jars lining the windows of Stan's Hardware, and <u>speculation</u> had to move on to Dolores. ❶

Dolores was the assistant manager at Stan's and had worked there for twenty years, since high school. She knew the store like a mother knows her baby, so Dick—who had trouble keeping up with things like prices and new brands of <u>drywall compound</u>—tried to keep himself busy in the back and give Dolores the run of the floor. This worked fine because the carpenters and plumbers and painters in town trusted Dolores and took her advice to heart. They also liked her tattoo.

Dolores was the only woman in town with a tattoo. On the days she went sleeveless, one could see it on the <u>taut</u> brown skin of her upper arm: "Howl at the Moon." The picture was of a baying coyote which must have been a dark gray in its early days but which had faded to the color of the <u>spackling paste</u> Dolores stocked in the third aisle. Nobody had gotten out of Dolores the true story behind the tattoo. Some of the men who came in liked to show off their own, and they'd roll up their sleeves or pull open their shirts, <u>exhibiting</u> bald eagles and rattlesnakes, and they'd try to coax out of Dolores the history of her coyote. All of the men

> ❶ **Comparing and Contrasting**
> How are Dolores and Dick alike? How are they different?

Vo•cab•u•lary

speculation (spek yoo LAY shun) contemplation or consideration of a subject

drywall compound (DRY wahl KAWM pownd) a paste used to patch holes in walls

taut (tawt) pulled or drawn tight; not slack

spackling paste (SPAK ling payst) a substance used to repair walls before painting

exhibiting (ek SIH bih ting) to show outwardly; display

had gotten their tattoos when they were in the service, drunk on weekend leave and full of the spitfire of young soldiers. Dolores had never been in the service and she'd never seen weekend leave and there wasn't a tattoo parlor anywhere near. They couldn't figure why or where any half-sober woman would have a howling coyote ground into the soft skin of her upper arm. But Dolores wasn't telling. ❷

That the flowers in Stan's front window had anything to do with Dolores seemed completely improbable. As far as anyone knew, Dolores had never been in love nor had anyone ever been in love with her. Some believed it was the tattoo, of course, or the fine dark hair coating Dolores's upper lip which kept suitors away. Some felt it was because Dolores was just more of a man than most of the men in town, and fellows couldn't figure out how to court someone who knew more about the carburetor of a car or the back side of a washing machine than they did. Others thought Dolores simply didn't want love. This was a popular theory among the women in town who sold Avon and Mary Kay cosmetics. Whenever one of them ran into the hardware for a package of light bulbs or some batteries, she would mentally pluck every one of the black hairs above Dolores's lip. Then she'd wash that grease out of Dolores's hair, give her a good blunt cut, dress her in a decent silk-blend blouse with a nice Liz Claiborne skirt from the Sports line, and, finally, tone down that swarthy, longshoreman look of Dolores's with a concealing beige foundation, some frosted peach lipstick, and a good gray liner for the eyes.

> **❷ Identifying Author's Perspective**
> How do you think the author feels about tattoos?

Vo•cab•u•lary

spitfire (SPIT fyr) a quick-tempered or highly excitable person
improbable (im PRAW buh bul) unlikely to take place or be true
carburetor (CAR bur ay tur) a device used in internal-combustion engines to produce an explosive mixture of vaporized fuel and air
swarthy (SWAHR thee) having a dark complexion or color
longshoreman (lawng SHOR muhn) a dock worker who loads and unloads ships

A Crush

Dolores simply didn't want love, the Avon lady would think as she walked back to her car carrying her little bag of batteries. If she did, she'd fix herself up.

The man who was in love with Dolores and who brought her zinnias and cornflowers and <u>nasturtiums</u> and marigolds and asters and four-o'clocks in clear mason jars did not know any of this. He did not know that men showed Dolores their tattoos. He did not know that Dolores understood how to use and to sell a belt sander. He did not know that Dolores needed some concealing beige foundation so she could get someone to love her. The man who brought flowers to Dolores on Wednesdays when the hardware opened its doors at 7:00 a.m. didn't care who Dolores had ever been or what anyone had ever thought of her. He loved her and he wanted to bring her flowers.

Ernie had lived in this town all of his life and had never before met Dolores. He was thirty-three years old, and for thirty-one of those years he had lived at home with his mother in a small, dark house on the edge of town near Beckwith's Orchards. Ernie had been a beautiful baby, with a shock of shining black hair and large blue eyes and a round, wise face. But as he had grown, it had become clearer and clearer that though he was indeed a perfectly beautiful child, his mind had not developed with the same perfection. Ernie would not be able to speak in sentences until he was six years old. He would not be able to count the apples in a bowl until he was eight. By the time he was ten, he could sing a simple song. At age twelve, he understood what a joke was. And when he was twenty, something he saw on television made him cry.

Ernie's mother kept him in the house with her because it was easier, so Ernie knew nothing of the world except this house. They lived, the two of them, in tiny dark rooms always

Vo•cab•u•lary

nasturtiums (nah STUR shumz) herbs with brightly colored flowers

illuminated by the glow of a television set, Ernie's bags of Oreos and Nutter Butters littering the floor, his baseball cards scattered across the sofa, his heavy winter coat thrown over the arm of a chair so he could wear it whenever he wanted, and his box of Burpee seed packages sitting in the middle of the kitchen table.

These Ernie cherished. The seeds had been delivered to his home by mistake. One day a woman wearing a brown uniform had pulled up in a brown truck, walked quickly to the front porch of Ernie's house, set a box down, and with a couple of toots of her horn, driven off again. Ernie had watched her through the curtains, and when she was gone, had ventured onto the porch and shyly, cautiously, picked up the box. His mother checked it when he carried it inside. The box didn't have their name on it but the brown truck was gone, so whatever was in the box was theirs to keep. Ernie pulled off the heavy tape, his fingers trembling, and found inside the box more little packages of seeds than he could count. He lifted them out, one by one, and examined the beautiful photographs of flowers on each. His mother was not interested, had returned to the television, but Ernie sat down at the kitchen table and quietly looked at each package for a long time, his fingers running across the slick paper and outlining the shapes of zinnias and cornflowers and nasturtiums and marigolds and asters and four-o'clocks, his eyes drawing up their colors.

Two months later Ernie's mother died. A neighbor found her at the mailbox beside the road. People from the county courthouse came out to get Ernie, and as they ushered him from the home he would never see again, he picked up the box of seed packages from his kitchen table and passed through the doorway.

Eventually Ernie was moved to a large white house near the main street of town. This house was called a group home, because in it lived a group of people who, like Ernie, could not live on their own. There were six of them. Each had his own

---

Vo•cab•u•lary

illuminated (il LOO muh nay ted) provided or brightened with light
ventured (VEN churd) proceeded despite possible danger or risk

room. When Ernie was shown the room that would be his, he put the box of Burpee seeds—which he had kept with him since his mother's death—on the little table beside the bed and then he sat down on the bed and cried.

Ernie cried every day for nearly a month. And then he stopped. He dried his tears and he learned how to bake refrigerator biscuits and how to dust mop and what to do if the indoor plants looked brown.

Ernie loved watering the indoor plants and it was this pleasure which finally drew him outside. One of the young men who worked at the group home—a college student named Jack—grew a large garden in the back of the house. It was full of tomato vines and the large yellow blossoms of healthy squash. During his first summer at the house, Ernie would stand at the kitchen window, watching Jack and sometimes a resident of the home move among the vegetables. Ernie was curious, but too afraid to go into the garden.

Then one day when Ernie was watching through the window, he noticed that Jack was ripping open several slick little packages and emptying them into the ground. Ernie panicked and ran to his room. But the box of Burpee seeds was still there on his table, untouched. He grabbed it, slid it under his bed, then went back through the house and out into the garden as if he had done this every day of his life.

He stood beside Jack, watching him empty seed packages into the soft black soil, and as the packages were emptied, Ernie asked for them, holding out his hand, his eyes on the photographs of red radishes and purple eggplant. Jack handed the empty packages over with a smile and with that gesture became Ernie's first friend. **3**

Jack tried to explain to Ernie that the seeds would grow into vegetables but Ernie could not believe this until he saw it come true. And when it did, he looked all the more <u>intently</u> at the packages of zinnias and cornflowers and the rest hidden beneath his bed. He thought more deeply about them but he could not carry them to the garden. He could not let the garden have his seeds.

That was the first year in the large white house.

The second year, Ernie saw Dolores, and after that he thought of nothing else but her and of the photographs of flowers beneath his bed.

Jack had decided to take Ernie downtown for breakfast every Wednesday morning to ease him into the world outside that of the group home. They left very early, at 5:45 a.m., so there would be few people and almost no traffic to frighten Ernie and make him beg for his room. Jack and Ernie drove to the Big Boy restaurant which sat across the street from Stan's Hardware. There they ate eggs and bacon and French toast among those whose work demanded rising before the sun: bus drivers, policemen, nurses, mill workers. Their first time in the Big Boy, Ernie was too nervous to eat. The second time, he could eat but he couldn't look up. The third time, he not only ate everything on his plate, but he lifted his head and he looked out the window of the Big Boy restaurant toward Stan's Hardware across the street. There he saw a dark-haired woman in jeans and a black

> **3 Comparing and Contrasting**
> Compare Ernie's life at the home with his life with his mother.

Vo•cab•u•lary

intently (in TENT lee) firmly fixed; concentrated

A Crush

T-shirt unlocking the front door of the building, and that was the moment Ernie started loving Dolores and thinking about giving up his seeds to the soft black soil of Jack's garden.

Love is such a mystery, and when it strikes the heart of one as mysterious as Ernie himself, it can hardly be spoken of. Ernie could not explain to Jack why he went directly to his room later that morning, pulled the box of Burpee seeds from under his bed, then grabbed Jack's hand in the kitchen and walked with him to the garden where Ernie had come to believe things would grow. Ernie handed the packets of seeds one by one to Jack, who stood in silent admiration of the lovely photographs before asking Ernie several times, "Are you sure you want to plant these?" Ernie was sure. It didn't take him very long, and when the seeds all lay under the moist black earth, Ernie carried his empty packages inside the house and spent the rest of the day spreading them across his bed in different arrangements.

That was in June. For the next several Wednesdays at 7:00 a.m., Ernie watched every movement of the dark-haired woman behind the lighted windows of Stan's Hardware. Jack watched Ernie watch Dolores, and <u>discreetly</u> said nothing.

When Ernie's flowers began growing in July, Ernie spent most of his time in the garden. He would watch the garden for hours, as if he expected it suddenly to move or to impress him with a quick trick. The fragile green stems of his flowers stood uncertainly in the soil, like baby colts on their first legs, but the young plants performed no magic for Ernie's eyes. They saved their shows for the middle of the night and the next day surprised Ernie with tender small blooms in all the colors the photographs had promised.

The flowers grew fast and <u>hardy</u>, and one early Wednesday morning when they looked as big and bright as their pictures on the empty packages, Ernie pulled a glass canning jar off a dusty

Vo•cab•u•lary
discreetly (dih SKREET lee) with discretion; prudently and with wise self-restraint
hardy (HAR dee) capable of surviving unfavorable conditions

shelf in the basement of his house. He washed the jar, half filled it with water, then carried it to the garden where he placed in it one of every kind of flower he had grown. He met Jack at the car and rode off to the Big Boy with the jar of flowers held tight between his small hands. Jack told him it was a beautiful bouquet.

When they reached the door of the Big Boy, Ernie stopped and pulled at Jack's arm, pointing to the building across the street. "OK," Jack said, and he led Ernie to the front door of Stan's Hardware. It was 6:00 a.m. and the building was still dark. Ernie set the clear mason jar full of flowers under the sign that read "Closed," then he smiled at Jack and followed him back across the street to get breakfast.

When Dolores arrived at seven and picked up the jar of zinnias and cornflowers and nasturtiums and marigolds and asters and four-o'clocks, Ernie and Jack were watching her from a booth in the Big Boy. Each had a wide smile on his face as Dolores put her nose to the flowers. Ernie giggled. They watched the lights of the hardware store come up and saw Dolores place the clear mason jar on the ledge of the front window. They drove home still smiling.

All the rest of that summer Ernie left a jar of flowers every Wednesday morning at the front door of Stan's Hardware. Neither Dick Wilcox nor Dolores could figure out why the flowers kept coming, and each of them assumed somebody had a crush on the other. But the flowers had an effect on them anyway. **4** Dick started spending more time out on the floor making conversation with the customers, while Dolores stopped wearing T-shirts to work and instead wore crisp white blouses with the sleeves rolled back off her wrists. Occasionally she put on a bracelet.

> **4 Comparing and Contrasting**
> Compare the effect the flowers had on Dick and Dolores.

By summer's end Jack and Ernie had become very good friends, and when the flowers in the garden behind their house began to wither, and Ernie's face began to grow gray as he watched them, Jack brought home one bright day in late September a great long box. Ernie followed Jack as he carried it down to the basement and watched as Jack pulled a long glass tube from the box and attached this tube to the wall above a table. When Jack plugged in the tube's electric cord, a soft lavender light washed the room.

"Sunshine," said Jack.

Then he went back to his car for a smaller box. He carried this down to the basement where Ernie still stood staring at the strange light. Jack handed Ernie the small box, and when Ernie opened it he found more little packages of seeds than he could count, with new kinds of photographs on the slick paper.

"Violets," Jack said, pointing to one of them.

Then he and Ernie went outside to get some dirt. ○

Answering the BIG Question

When you do the following activities, consider the Big Question:
Who influences us and how do they do so?

WRITE TO LEARN What or who influenced the characters in the story to change? Make a chart like the following to record your answers in your Learner's Notebook.

PARTNER TALK Discuss your thoughts about the characters with a classmate who has read this selection.

Character	Change	What caused the change?
Dolores		
Dick		
Ernie		

R. L. Stine

by Christine M. Hill

He's the writer who knows how to give you the chills every time you open his books!

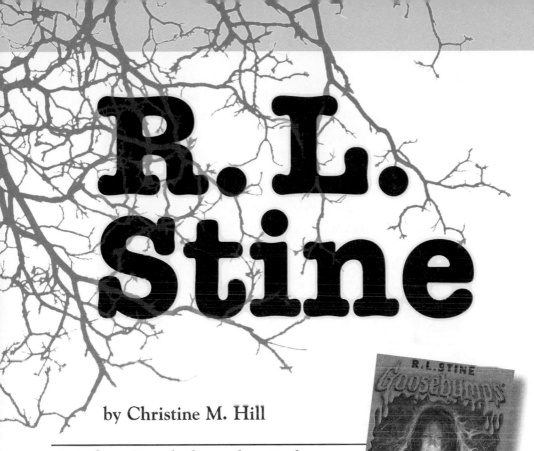

Three-year-old Bob Stine settled down for his afternoon nap. His mother read him a chapter of his favorite book, *Pinocchio*, as she did every day. Little Bob hung on every word as the wooden puppet in the story sat down and put his feet up on the stove. When the puppet fell asleep, his wooden feet burned off! Mrs. Stine was not reading from the sweetened Walt Disney movie version of the story. She was reading the original tale by Carlo Collodi. It was "gruesome," R. L. Stine remembers. "Very <u>influential</u> in my writing."

Vo•cab•u•lary

influential (in floo EN shull) having power to affect others

Robert Laurence Stine was born on October 8, 1943, in Columbus, Ohio. His father, Lewis, worked for a restaurant supply company, and his mother, Anne, was a homemaker. Eventually, Bob had a brother, Bill, three years younger, and a sister, Pam, seven years younger. The Stines lived in Bexley, Ohio, a wealthy suburb of Columbus. Though their house was smaller than their neighbors' houses and their lifestyle more modest, Lewis and Anne Stine provided a happy, comfortable life for their children. Bob had normal childhood fears—big dogs, swimming lessons, the dark, forbidden attic. "Nothing too scary," he says. But from an early age, he loved to give himself goose bumps. The Stines did not buy a television set until Bob was nine. Before that, he spent hours listening to plays on the radio.

Every week, he tuned in to a radio show called *Suspense*. It began with the sound of a gong, then a deep, chilling voice slowly announced, "And now . . . tales . . . calculated . . . to keep you . . . in suspense!" Bob was so terrified by the show's introduction that he flicked the radio off and never listened to a single episode. "Today, I try to make my books as scary as that announcer's voice," he says. ❶

When Bob was in grade school, he found an old typewriter. With one finger, he began to pound out stories, comics, and magazines. Bob's first magazine was called *The All New Bob Stine Giggle Book*. He still owns the only copy, which measures three inches by four inches.

❶ **Identifying Author's Purpose**
What does the author want to tell you about young Bob?

Bob's writing models were *Mad* magazine and the gory DC horror comics, including *Tales from the Crypt*. His mother forbade him to bring these home, declaring them "trash." Luckily, Bob discovered that they were available at the barbershop. Every week, he read his favorite magazines from cover to cover before getting a quick trim. "As a result, I had even less hair than I do now," he says.

Even when he was a kid, writing was Bob's passion. He scored B's on his report card without much study. His main interest in school was getting laughs by making jokes and passing around his homemade humor comics. What did his parents make of this? "They kept telling me to go out and play!" he says. But secretly they were proud. At thirteen, Bob had his bar mitzvah service, becoming an adult in the Jewish faith. As a gift, his parents gave him a heavy-duty, office-quality typewriter, just what he wanted. In high school, he told them he could not get a summer job because he was writing a novel. The Stines accepted this explanation without question.

Bob graduated from high school in Bexley in 1961. For college, he chose Ohio State University in nearby Columbus. Not only could he live at home, he could write for Ohio State's famous humor magazine, *Sundial*. After a year of writing for the magazine, sometimes producing entire issues by himself, Stine became editor in chief. He held the post for three years.

After graduating from Ohio State in 1965, Stine wanted to move to New York City. "I figured that's where writers lived," he

said. To save money for the move, Stine became a high school substitute teacher. He used the experience to eavesdrop on students' conversations. He credits this year with giving him a good ear for how kids really talk. He also enjoyed swapping comic books with his students.

Stine's goal when he moved to New York in 1966 was to edit his own humor magazine. To gain experience, he first worked for some other magazines, relating investment advice, inventing celebrity interviews, and reporting on soft-drink industry news. Finally, in 1968, he went to work at Scholastic Press magazines, where he would stay for sixteen years.

Meanwhile, at a party on a rainy night, Stine met a beautiful redhead with a terrible cold, Jane Waldhorn. Despite her sniffles, they fell in love. They were married on June 22, 1969.

Stine began his career at Scholastic writing and editing social studies articles. He thrived on the fast pace of weekly magazines. Magazine work does not allow for writer's block, he says, and attributes his ability to write fast to his Scholastic years. Jane Stine also became a Scholastic magazine editor.

After several years, Bob Stine founded and edited a teen humor magazine for Scholastic called *Bananas*. It featured movie <u>parodies</u>, advice given by a dog, and a character named Phil Fly, who begged in every issue not to be swatted. Later, Stine edited a similar magazine called *Maniac*. Though his lifelong dream of editing a humor magazine was fulfilled, Stine had not reached the peak of his career.

While working at *Bananas*, Stine received a call from a children's book editor at E. P. Dutton. She asked if he might like to write a humorous children's book for her. Stine decided to write a book he would have found useful as a kid. He filled *How to Be Funny* with tips and quizzes for budding jokesters.

The Stines' only child, Matthew, was born in 1980. When

Vo•cab•u•lary

parodies (PAIR uh deez) funny imitations

Matthew was little, Stine spent a great deal of time exploring New York with his son. After Scholastic's humor magazines went out of business, Stine worked at home writing children's books. "I don't want a job [when I grow up]," said Matthew. "I want to hang around the house like Dad."

In 1982, Stine became head writer for the children's television show *Eureeka's Castle*. He and his team wrote humorous sketches for the show's cast of puppets. Stine based one of the puppet characters, Batly, on his son. Whenever Batly fell down or ran into something, which was often, he, like Matthew, would jump up and shout, "I meant to do that!" After Stine's staff produced one hundred hours of programming, however, they lost their jobs. No new shows would be made. The original shows would simply be rerun.

Stine resumed writing at home. He produced dozens of joke books, adventure novels in which readers can choose different plotlines, and series books based on television shows, movies, and even toys.

One day, Stine had lunch with a friend who was an editor at Scholastic Books. Horror novels for teenagers were growing in popularity, she said. Why didn't he try his hand at one? She even gave him a title—*Blind Date*. Stine went home and started plotting. *Blind Date* took a month to outline and three months to write, which was slow for Stine. "I didn't really know what I was doing," Stine admits. When it was published in 1986, this story of a boy harassed by phone calls from a dead girl claiming to be his blind date was a smash hit.

Stine followed it up with three more horror novels: *Twisted*, in 1987; *Broken Date*, in 1988; and *The Babysitter*, in 1989. Then his wife asked him to write a horror series for her new publishing company. Jane Stine had quit her editorial job to start Parachute Press. Bob Stine came up with a series title, *Fear Street*. "Where your worst nightmares live," Jane promptly answered when he proposed it to her.

The *Fear Street* books began appearing in 1989. There are more than one hundred titles in print. Stine still writes them at the rate of one a month, and they are one of the most popular teen paperback series in America.

So many younger kids wanted to read *Fear Street* that Stine began a new series for them in 1992—*Goosebumps*. The books were an immediate sensation. ❷ Even with their cliffhanger chapter endings and roller-coaster-like suspense, Stine believes the stories are "safe scares." He adds, "I'm very careful never to make these books too REAL. . . . [I] keep many real-world problems, such as drug abuse or alcoholism, out."

Stine also writes one *Goosebumps* book a month. Luckily, he never lacks for ideas. Sometimes just a single image gives him his idea. The mental picture of a bathtub full of worms suggested

> ❷ **Distinguishing Fact from Opinion**
> Can the author's statements be proven?

Go Eat Worms. Sometimes real events are the trigger. One Halloween, Matthew Stine wore a green rubber Frankenstein mask. When he could not take it off, Stine had his inspiration for *The Haunted Mask.*

Goosebumps is the top-selling young people's book series in history, with more than two hundred million copies in print. Stine followed it with the *Goosebumps 2000* series in 1998. It has inspired a television series, toys, and a ride at Disney-MGM Studios. The books have even been packed into bags of Doritos tortilla chips.

Stine receives more than one thousand fan letters a week. Many of them are from parents thanking him for turning their kids into readers. These kids, particularly boys, never read anything before they encountered R. L. Stine. "I'm very proud of the fact that I created something to help get boys reading," he says. One boy who never reads R. L. Stine is his son, Matthew. "He knows it drives me CRAZY!" says his dad.

Though he has no plans to retire, Stine knows that the *Goosebumps* <u>phenomenon</u> cannot last forever. In fact, "I'm sort of counting on it [ending]," he says. "Then I can take it easy." ○

Answering the BIG Question

When you do the following activities, consider the Big Question:
Who influences us and how do they do so?

WRITE TO LEARN Many people influenced R. L. Stine's writing career. Who do you think were the two biggest influences and why? Write a persuasive paragraph in your Learner's Notebook to answer these questions.

LITERATURE GROUPS Share and discuss your paragraph with two or three classmates who have read the selection.

Vo•cab•u•lary

phenomenon (fuh NAWM uh nawn) an exceptional thing

Index of Authors and Titles

Acknowledgments

Literature credits

Unit 1

"The Calamity Kids in the Bermuda Triangle Terrarium!" by Jerzy Drozd and Sara Turner.

"To Young Readers" by Gwendolyn Brooks. Reprinted by consent of Brooks Permissions.

"Invitation" from *Where the Sidewalk Ends* by Shel Silverstein. Copyright © 1974 by Evil Eye Music. Reprinted by permission of HarperCollins.

"Real Spider Superpowers" by Sarah Ives. *National Geographic KidsNews*, July 6, 2004. Reprinted by permission of the National Geographic Society.

"Blues for Bob E. Brown" by T. Ernesto Bethancourt, copyright © 1993 by T. Ernesto Bethancourt. From *Big City Cool* edited by M. Jerry Weiss and Helen S. Weiss. Copyright © 2002 M. Jerry Weiss and Helen M. Weiss. Reprinted by permission of Persea Books.

"Hurricane Emily bad news for endangered turtles" by Eloise Quintanilla. From the *Chicago Sun-Times* Friday, July 22, 2005.

"Naked Animals" by David George Gordon. *National Geographic KidsNews*. Reprinted by permission of the National Geographic Society.

"Animal House" by Heather Herman, as told to Louise Jarvis. From *Teen Vogue* September 2004. Edited by Alyssa Giacobbe.

"King Tut's Mysterious Death" by Kristin Baird Rattini. *National Geographic KidsNews*. Reprinted by permission of the National Geographic Society.

Unit 2

"The No-Guitar Blues" from *Baseball in April and Other Stories* by Gary Soto. Copyright © 1990 by Gary Soto. Reprinted in *Help Wanted: Short Stories about Young People Working* selected by Anita Silvey. Reprinted by permission of Little, Brown and Company.

"Merrick Johnston: Mountain Climber" from *Gutsy Girls: Young Women Who Dare* by Tina Schwager, P. T. A., A. T. C., and Michele Schuerger © 1999. Used with permission from Free Spirit Publishing Inc., Minneapolis, MN; 1-866-703-7322; www.freespirit.com. All rights reserved.

"Krumping: If You Look Like Bozo Having Spasms, You're Doing It Right" by Shaheem Reid with additional reporting by Mark Bella for MTV News. Copyright © 2005 by MTV Networks.

"Chicago Kids Sink Their Teeth Into Dino Camp" by Sarah Ives. *National Geographic KidsNews*, July 20, 2004. Reprinted by permission of the National Geographic Society.

"Asteroid Belt" by Steven Maxwell.

"Caterpillars" from *If Only I Could Fly* (Boyds Mills Press, 1984). From *The Beauty of the Beast: Poems from the Animal Kingdom* selected by Jack Prelutsky. Selection copyright © 1997 by Jack Prelutsky. Reprinted by permission of Alfred A. Knopf.

"The Girl Who Makes the Cymbals Bang," copyright © 1991 by X. J. Kennedy. First appeared in *The Kite That Braves Old Orchard Beach*, published by Margaret K. McElderry Books. Reprinted by permission of Curtis Brown, Ltd.

"The Race" by Jennifer Trujillo, a poem from the collection *Love to Mama: A Tribute to Mothers*. Text copyright © 2001 by Jennifer Trujillo. Permission arranged with Lee & Low Books Inc., New York, NY, 10016.

"A Determined Pair" from *Promises To Keep: How Jackie Robinson Changed America* by Sharon Robinson. Copyright © 2004 by Sharon Robinson. Reprinted by permission of Scholastic Press.

"The Dog Diaries" copyright © 1992 by Merrill Markoe. From *What the Dogs Have Taught Me*. Reprinted with permission by Melanie Jackson Agency, LLC.

"It's Not A Crime To Love Science" by Juliann F. Willey, from *33 Things Every Girl Should Know: Stories, Songs, Poems, and Smart Talk by 33 Extraordinary Women*, edited by Tonya Bolden. Copyright © 1998 by Tonya Bolden. Reprinted by permission of Crown Publishers, a division of Random House, Inc.

"Hollywood and the Pits," copyright © 1992 by Cherylene Lee. Reprinted by permission of Bret Adams Ltd.

Unit 3

"Raymond's Run" copyright © 1971 by Toni Cade Bambara, from *Gorilla, My Love* by Toni Cade Bambara. Used by permission of Random House, Inc.

"Tales of a Seventh Grade Nada" by Bizet Kizcorn.

Lou Gehrig's farewell speech and "To Lou Gehrig" TM/© Estate of Eleanor Gehrig by CMG Worldwide/www.LouGehrig.com. Reprinted by permission.

"A Song for Momma" from the album *Evolution* by Boyz II Men. Produced by Babyface. Copyright © 1997.

"Sister/Friend" by April Halprin Wayland, from *Girl Coming in for a Landing: A Novel in Poems*. Copyright © 2002 by April Halprin Wayland. Alfred A. Knopf.

"Poem" from *The Collected Poems of Langston Hughes* by Langston Hughes, copyright © 1994 by The Estate of Langston Hughes. Used by permission of Alfred A. Knopf, a division of Random House, Inc.

Excerpt from *The Fellowship of the Ring* by J. R. R. Tolkien. Copyright © 1954, 1965 by J. R. R. Tolkien. Copyright © renewed 1982 by Christopher R. Tolkien, Michael H. R. Tolkien, John F. R. Tolkien, and Priscilla M. A. R. Tolkien. Copyright © renewed 1993 by Christopher R. Tolkien, John F. R. Tolkien, and Priscilla M. A. R. Tolkien. Reprinted by permission of Houghton Mifflin Company. All rights reserved.

"Hobbit-like Human Ancestor Found" by Hillary Mayell. *National Geographic KidsNews*, November 22, 2004. Reprinted by permission of the National Geographic Society.

From *Anne Frank: The Diary of a Young Girl* by Anne Frank. Copyright © 1952 by Otto H. Frank. Used by permission of Doubleday, a division of Bantam Doubleday Dell Publishing Group, Inc.

"Baby Hippo Orphan Finds a Friend" by Catherine Clarke Fox. From *National Geographic Kids*, March 4, 2005 copyright © 2005 by the National Geographic Society.

When the Rattlesnake Sounds by Alice Childress. Copyright © 1975 by Alice Childress. From *Best Plays: 7 Plays for Young People*, edited by Patricia Opaskar and Mary Ann Trost, copyright © 1998 by NTC/Contemporary Publishing Group, Inc. Reprinted by permission of Jamestown Publishers.

Unit 4

"The Day I Ran with Lance Armstrong" by Samuel Brook Douglas. *Skipping Stones* March-April 2005. Reprinted by permission of *Skipping Stones* Magazine.

From "Ice Cube—Actor/Musician" by McClain J. and Angela R. Reprinted with permission of *Teen Ink* and TeenInk.com.

"Third Down and Forever" by Douglas Holgate.

"Dealing with Peer Pressure." This information was provided by KidsHealth, one of the largest resources online for medically reviewed health information written for parents, kids, and teens. For more articles like this one, visit www.KidsHealth.org or www.TeensHealth.org.

"Thanking the Birds" by Joseph Bruchac. Reprinted by permission of Barbara S. Kouts.

"Whose Reality Are We Talking About?" feature edited by Antionetta Kelley and Tanasia White. From *Teen Voices* Volume 14 Issue 1. Copyright © 2005 by Women Express, Inc.

"Jimmy Jet and His TV Set" from *Where The Sidewalk Ends* by Shel Silverstein. Copyright © 1974 by Evil Eye Music. Reprinted by permission of HarperCollins.

Acknowledgments

"A Gold Miner's Tale" from *We The People: Poems by Bobbi Katz*, by Bobbi Katz. Copyright © 1998, 2000 by Bobbi Katz. Reprinted by permission of Greenwillow Books, an imprint of HarperCollins Publishers.

"Waiting for the War" by Graham Salisbury. From *Time Capsule: Short Stories About Teenagers Throughout the Twentieth Century*, edited by Donald R. Gallo. Story copyright © 1999 by Graham Salisbury. Reprinted by permission of Delacorte Press, a division of Random House, Inc.

"The Struggle to Be an All-American Girl" by Elizabeth Wong. Reprinted by permission of the author, www.elizabethwong.net.

"A Crush" from *A Couple of Kooks and Other Stories About Love* by Cynthia Rylant. Published by Scholastic Inc./Orchard Books. Copyright © 1990 by Cynthia Rylant. Reprinted by permission.

"R. L. Stine" from *Ten Terrific Authors for Teens* by Christine M. Hill. Copyright © 2000 by Christine M. Hill. Reprinted by permission of Enslow Publishers, Inc.

Glencoe would like to acknowledge the artists who participated in illustrating this program: Sara Turner and Jerzy Drozd; Donovan Foote; Steven Murray; Bizet Kizkorn; Douglas Holgate.

Photo credits

Cover (cl)Darren Hopes/Getty Images, (t)Index Stock Imagery, (bl)Brand X Pictures/PunchStock, (cr)Sara Turner & Jerzy Drozd, (br)Nick Koudis/Getty Images; **0** (inset)Rubberball/Getty Images, (bkgd)MBCheatham/iStock International, others Greg Paprocki/Getty Images; **14** Medioimages/Getty Images; **16** 2006 Jupiterimages Corporation; **17 18 19** Index Stock Imagery; **23** Stockbyte/Getty Images; **25** Darren Hopes/Getty Images; **28** CORBIS; **32** Darren Hopes/Getty Images; **35** Index Stock Imagery; **38** NOAA; **39** Digital Vision/Getty Images; **40** Henry Ausloos/Animals Animals; **42** (bkgd)Index Stock Imagery, Diane Diederich/iStock Photo; **45** David Zalubowski/AP/Wide World Photos; **46** Ryan McVay/Getty Images; **47** Brand X Pictures/PunchStock, (bkgd)CORBIS, Brand X Pictures/PunchStock; **71** SW Productions/Getty Images; **72** Rubberball; **77** (r)Getty Images, (l)Rubberball; **80** Alan Pappe/Getty Images; **81** (bkgd)Comstock, Courtesy Merrick Johnston; **87** Dynamic Graphics/2006 Jupiterimages Corporation; **89** Courtesy Tommy the Clown; **91** Kevork Djansezian/AP/Wide World Photos; **93** CORBIS; **94 95** Conor Barnes/Project Exploration; **108** (bkgd)Harnett/Hanzon/Getty Images, CORBIS; **111** Getty Images; **113** AP/Wide World Photos; **114** RKO Radio Pictures; **116** AP/Wide World Photos; **118** (inset)Digital Vision, Rubberball; **121** (l)Ryan McVey/Getty Images, (c)(r)Getty Images; **124** Creatas; **127** (bkgd)Digital Vision, Nick Koudis/Getty Images; **129** (bkgd)Comstock, CORBIS; **132** CORBIS; **133** Courtesy Cherylene Lee; **134 136 137 138** CORBIS; **139** Nicholas Pitt/Getty Images; **140** CORBIS; **142** 2006 Jupiterimages Corporation; **143** CORBIS; **167** Bettmann/CORBIS; **169** Don Tremain/Getty Images; Trinette Reed/Brand X Pictures/2006 Jupiterimages Corporation; **171** Rubberball/Getty Images; **172** CORBIS; **173** Kurt Strazdins/Knight-Ridder/Tribune Media Information Services; **178** Knight-Ridder/Tribune Media Information Services; **183** Stephen Hird/Reuters/CORBIS; **185** Reuters/CORBIS; **187** Comstock; **189 191** CORBIS; **197** Louie Psihoyos/CORBIS; **201** CORBIS; **202** Keith Philpott/Time Life Pictures/Getty Images; **205** USDA; **206** Brant Sanderlin/Atlanta Journal-Constitution; **208** C Squared Studios/Getty Images; **209** Jules Frazier/Getty Images; **210** Index Stock Imagery, Karl Walter/Getty Images; **212** Peter Kramer/Getty Images; **227** Stockbyte; **229** Maria Taglienti-Molinari/Brand X Pictures/2006 Jupiterimages Corporation; **232** 2006 Jupiterimages Corporation; **233** Rubberball; **234** C Squared Studios/Getty Images; **237** Jules Frazier/Getty Images; **238** S. Solum/PhotoLink/Getty Images; **247** Hot Ideas; **249** Getty Images; **255** Marjory Collins/Getty Images; **257** Getty Images; **259 261** 2006 Jupiterimages Corporation; **263 264 265** Siede Preis/Getty Images; **266** CORBIS; **269** Siede Preis/Getty Images; **271** Illustration by Tim Jacobus from GOOSEBUMPS: BE CAREFUL WHAT YOU WISH FOR by R.L. Stine. Illustration copyright © by Parachute Press, Inc. Reprinted by permission of Scholastic Inc.; **276** From GOOSEBUMPS - SERIES 2000: THE WEREWOLF IN THE LIVING ROOM by R.L. Stine. Copyright © 1999 by Parachute Press, Inc. Reprinted by permission of Scholastic Inc. GOOSEBUMPS is a registered trademark of Parachute Press; **276** ImageSource/2006 Jupiterimages Corporation.